"Fear rose within me as I anticipated taking the step. It was a step that would take me into my shadow, a step that would illuminate the darkness of being and allow me to experience the light of creation."

ENDORSEMENTS

"A deep immersion into the mysterious teachings of the Andes from an explorer and doctor who becomes a shaman. Riveting, mind-boggling, and enchanting as we follow the steps and lessons to becoming a man of wisdom and power. Use it as your guide and compass!"

> Alberto Villoldo, PhD
> Bestselling author of *Shaman, Healer, Sage,* and *One Spirit Medicine*

"This book is the richest source of wisdom I have come across in a long time, filled with inspiration and alive with healing energy; an incredible resource for the modern healer."

> Joe Tafur, MD
> Author of *The Fellowship of the River:*
> *A Medical Doctor's Exploration into Traditional Amazonian Plant Medicine*

"A sharing of timeless wisdom and knowledge. A must-read for those walking the path to health and wholeness! This book is the medicine for your journey."

> Julie A. Hannon, MA
> Shamanic practitioner and teacher

OF INTEGRATION
AND
UNDERSTANDING
THE JOURNEY

OF INTEGRATION AND UNDERSTANDING THE JOURNEY

THE JOURNEY HAS SERVED US.
NOW LET US SERVE THE JOURNEY.

JAMES K. DEWELL, M.D.

ISBN: 978-1-7343342-1-0 (Paperback)
ISBN: 978-1-7343342-0-3 (Hardcover)
ISBN: 978-1-7343342-2-7 (eBook)

Library of Congress Control Number: 2019919706

Front cover image with permission Luis Rumy Salinas Quispe

Images by James Dewell
Additional images with permission Lynn Berryhill and Luis Rumy Salinas Quispe
Book Cover Design by ebooklaunch.com
First printing edition 2020

Published by:
James K. Dewell
La Canada, California 91011

James.K.Dewell@gmail.com

Contents

ACKNOWLEDGMENTS

My special gratitude goes out to Lynn Berryhill, Deborah Wray, Marcela Lobos, Oliver Cooperman, Dean Taraborelli, Peter Bonaker, Ruby Parker, Elise Kost, Karen Hoza, Julie Hannon, and Terry Rhodes.

I thank Linda Fitch, former dean of the Four Winds Society's Healing the Light Body School, and each of the teachers, assistants, and students who I have encountered on this journey.

I thank and offer my gratitude to each client who has allowed me the great honor of participating in their journey of healing and illumination, as they, too, have been my teachers.

I also offer my thanks to our four-legged friends, especially Bear, Fetch, Cassanova, and Ralph, who have been the true healers for many.

Alberto, great blessings to you for your friendship, your guidance, and your willingness to share the wisdom and teachings of this journey with me.

To my wife, Jemela, and my daughter, Alicia, who have walked this path with me, I offer my countless thanks, gratitude, and a stone for their journey.

Finally, I offer this work in dedication to the medicine men and women who have come before, are with us now, and those who will come after.

PREFACE

For those who wish to assimilate the wisdom and transform their life, it would be my suggestion to obtain a journal. Then as you read through the pages that follow, make notes about that which resonates with you or that which does not. Allow time to process your experience and the wisdom and the teachings found within this work. Then when ready, from a place of honesty and without judgment, go back and perform the exercises and answer the questions that arise from within or outside the pages of this book.

Listen to the answers. Sit with the answers. Ask questions of the answers. Allow the questions and answers to bring clarity and understanding to the journey we call life.

****

Note: Shamanic healing is complementary to, not a replacement for, Western medicine. If you are currently under the care of a physician, do not stop or alter any therapy or prescription usage without first consulting your physician or health-care provider. It may also be appropriate to consult with a physician or therapist as you process the information within this guide.

****

INTRODUCTION

OF INTEGRATION AND UNDERSTANDING THE JOURNEY

Perhaps I began this journey when I was three, that summer day as I looked down upon my body floating two feet beneath the surface of the crystal-clear waters of Lake Tahoe. To this day, it remains unclear who freed me as I was submerged beneath the inner tube.

My connection to nature and animals began early on. When I was a toddler, there was the dog that would jump into the crib with me as I napped. There were the bluebirds who would watch over me as my mother went to pick up my sisters from school. There were the trees that I would climb. The stones that would call to me, and that I collected along the way.

This undertaking did not begin as a book. It began as a way for me to remember, to understand, to make sense of the journey I was on. As I documented the journey, this attempt to understand began to transform into a book. A book of shared wisdom and of shared knowledge. A book that has transcended my own personal journey, and that has transformed into a guide that might assist others as they journey for awareness and understanding.

It is not my intention to present the entirety of the exercises or the wisdom found within this book as my personal creation. My shamanic training has been greatly influenced by Alberto Villoldo, PhD, founder of both the Fourwinds Society and the Healing the Light Body School. Many of the healing practices presented in this book are a synthesis and integration of my experience and interpretation of the wisdom and the healing practices that Alberto has shared and taught in the Healing the Light Body School. Many are not.

Where possible I have experienced the healing practices in the indigenous settings, directly from the medicine men and women who have served as the keepers of this wisdom. I have tried to maintain the integrity of these teachings and present them as I experienced them, without infringing upon proprietary materials or cultural appropriation.

The medicine and the teachings are not ours. We are the carriers of the medicine. We do not own the medicine; it is not ours to own. I thank the lineages of medicine men and women, past, present, and future, who have allowed us to walk with them on this path. These are the ones who have shared the ancient wisdom and knowledge that we may continue to serve the medicine as we walk the path of the healer.

PART ONE

OF INTEGRATION AND UNDERSTANDING

THE JOURNEY BEGINS

CHAPTER ONE

ESALEN

It was a year ago this month, February 2006, that Terry called and asked me to accompany him to Esalen. There was a workshop on shamanism. Of course I would go. Why not? My intent, though, was to spend the weekend at Esalen in the water of the hot springs that overlook the Pacific Ocean. Terry, well, Terry could attend the workshop.

The Esalen Institute, founded in the early sixties as a spiritual retreat center, became the birthplace of the human potential movement—a movement that attracted as lecturers and faculty at Esalen the likes of Aldous Huxley, Abraham Maslow, Joseph Campbell, Linus Pauling, Timothy Leary, Bob Dylan, Joni Mitchell, and Joan Baez to name a few. It was a movement to empower the individual self, a movement to meet the self in the here and the now. It was seen as an opportunity to expand the awareness of self beyond the unconscious boundaries we create. It was a means to fully access the innate potential available within us. It was a movement to create harmony, awareness, and wholeness at the level of body, mind, spirit, and soul.

For thousands of years the indigenous peoples have known of the sacred waters at Esalen and of these enchanted lands—lands that have been home to ancient gatherings and that have offered their gifts of joy and beauty to souls seeking health, harmony, and wholeness. Today, just as thousands of years ago, those seeking nourishment and healing for the body, mind, and soul continue to come together to experience the lands and waters of Esalen. I, too, was returning to be nourished by the essence of these lands and soak in the sacred waters.

* * *

I call. The workshop is full, but there is room for a personal retreat if we so desire. For me the hot springs are the real draw. We continue north along the coast to Big Sur. Upon arriving at the front guard shack, we are directed to the main office. We are told, "Two spaces opened this morning for the shamanism workshop, and we have held them for you." Hmmm ... for fifty dollars more ... the hot springs and perhaps a few minutes with the shaman. Not a bad trade-off!

Terry has already bought this dude's book and is now reading in the room. Not me. I drop my suitcase and my clothes, then head for the hot springs. But first I stop to cleanse at one of the two most beautiful showers in the world: a communal shower that opens to the great Pacific Ocean.

The rain, already begun, will continue well into the night and throughout the weekend. Slowly I slip into the warm waters of the springs, taking in the beauty of the setting and of the naked bodies that share the waters with me. Shortly, the first of many whales appears in the ocean.

A few hours later I return to the room. Terry, reading from Alberto's book about shamanism, greets me with the news that shamans are people of percept. My response: "Thanks. Would you like a glass of wine before dinner?" The wine always seems to help the meals at Esalen. I notice that even the hardened vegetarians have a glass or two before dinner. Perhaps the wine just tastes good. Surveying the scene at dinner, I notice several of the naked bodies from the hot springs earlier. They look different in clothes, some much nicer, others worse.

It is still raining. Perhaps raining is an understatement. The wind is gusting well over sixty miles per hour. The lightning is almost constant, and the rain a downpour. We walk the half mile or so to the big yurt where Alberto Villoldo will speak. I know his name now as most of those attending Esalen this weekend are here to hear him speak. The yurt is located on a bluff maybe fifty feet from the ocean. There are perhaps a hundred people of all ages and genders already present as we enter. Terry and I sit on the floor.

A few minutes later a young man, dressed in animal skins and holding a rattle, walks through the door. "Hi. Alberto will not be here tonight. I am the shaman from the Post Ranch Inn." For the next hour we hear about what Alberto would have told us had he been here. Alberto this, Alberto that. I look at Terry and say, "If you want to find me tomorrow, I will be in the hot springs."

"Okay, time to go out and offer that which no longer serves us to the fire," says the shaman. After watching this guy, I know why shamanism has a bad name. We all slowly put on our rain gear and circle around the firepit. "To the winds of the South," he begins, and within seconds the rain stops. The clouds clear. The sky is black now save the stars and the moon. For the next hour we chant and burn the sticks into which we have blown our fear, our anger, and our limiting beliefs. We stand behind our brothers and sisters to protect them from the unseen as they make their offerings to this sacred fire.

An hour has passed. Our prayers and offerings to the fire are complete. The shaman gives thanks and gratitude to the spirits who have held space for us tonight. The ceremonial space is now closed.

There had been no rain, wind, or lightning during the ceremony. Now within moments the wind and rain return and are fierce. The clouds carried by these winds obscure the stars and the moon. The cleansing rains fall hard to the ground, and near constant lightning illuminates the darkness of this night. The shaman announces Alberto will be here in the morning. I whisper to Terry, "I definitely won't be."

By 6 a.m. I am back in the springs. A few other naked bodies that I now recognize from the workshop are there as well. All comment on the events of last night: "Alberto had better be there today or we are leaving." I go back to get Terry at the room, but he has already gone to the dining hall and is sipping coffee. I let him know I will be found in the tubs for the rest of the weekend. But as we leave breakfast, I walk with him and end up at the yurt.

Alberto, a man in his mid-fifties, looks quite normal. There are no animal skins. He's wearing jeans, a green shirt, and a down vest, not unlike how I am dressed. He tells us of the weekend to come. We will learn about and experience the art and practice of soul retrievals, extractions, illuminations, and energy cutting. All of this sounds extremely weird, very new age, and a complete waste of time. Certainly does not interest me, as I ask of myself, *How do I get out to the springs without being obvious?* Oh, did I say that out loud? Alberto looks at me, and suggests I come to the front so that he can demonstrate energy cutting.

Okay, up I go. "Now just put your arms out in front of you, and don't let me push down." No problem. Yep, I am strong. The arms don't move. A second later, with a passing of his hand a few inches in front of me, my arms drop, no strength. He repairs his action and now I am again strong. I am hooked.

As the day progresses we hear about the healing power of stones, of journeying to the underworld to retrieve our lost soul parts, of journeying to the upper world to change our destiny, and then it is time to unblock and balance our chakras.

Terry and I work together. As Terry works on me, I am quite relaxed but soon have a vision of an ancient African warrior holding a golden shield blocking whatever is being done to me. Thirty minutes later Terry arouses me. "Okay, I give up," he says. "Something, someone, was blocking me, and there was no way to balance the chakras." I tell him of my vision.

Throughout the day and whenever there is a break, I migrate to the tubs. The nights are beautiful despite the continuing rain. The moon and stars occasionally peek out. There is a small group of us who still would rather be in the tubs than in the lectures, but something continues to pull us back to the lectures.

Over the past twenty years, I have never seen whales off the coast of Big Sur. Now there are pods breaching the waters everywhere.

The evening session begins. Alberto is speaking. Tonight, we will learn about intrusive energy. We will learn how to track for intrusive energies and entities in each other. An intrusive energy is heavy energy which takes on a consciousness that may guide us into a reality of disempowerment. Entities are disincarnated souls who have entered our energetic field and attached themselves to our chakras. We learn that they are not bad but can affect us adversely.

Marcela, a beautiful Chilean lady in her thirties, demonstrates how to track for an intrusive energy within another. Oddly, the person she performs the demonstration on has not been seen in the conference previously (yes, must be a ringer), and of course this poor soul has an entity that must be removed. How convenient. Now we test each other. I test Terry. He shows no evidence of a disincarnate being present within him, but then who will, I think. Terry tests me.

I am unable to resist his lightest touch. Alberto asks, "Well, anybody have an entity?" No one raises their hands, and neither do I.

As the evening class ends, I approach Alberto and say, "I have an entity, what next?"

He says, "Well, you could call Marcela. Oh, but she will be in Chile. Well, call her anyway. She will take care of you."

Oh sure, I think.

The conference concludes on Sunday. As we head south to Los Angeles, twenty to thirty whales breach the surface, as if to say goodbye. Terry and I talk.

My recollection is how familiar this all felt and that I was coming home.

CHAPTER TWO

HOME

It had been a week since returning home from Esalen. The rain continued. It was cold. The fire in our living room was warm. My back was facing the fireplace when the smoke first appeared. There from the right side of my torso, dark grayish black smoke. My hand went to my side, but there was no heat to be felt. Stepping away I looked at the fire. It was smokeless.

Without much thought I moved back in front of the fireplace. The smoke once again billowed as a cloud from the right side of my abdomen. After the third time this happened within a five-minute period, I climbed to the roof in the pouring rain to check the chimney, but there was no blockage and the only smoke was going straight up the flue.

There was only one place where this smoke could have originated, and I was not going to tell anyone and certainly did not want to believe it myself. That afternoon I ordered Alberto's book *Shaman, Healer, Sage.*

Over the ensuing months, many strange and indescribable events occurred. I was happy when the hummingbirds arrived that spring, all 250 of them, and stayed in our front yard for several weeks because then I could talk to people and comment, "Well, we certainly have lots of hummingbirds this year. Unusual, isn't it?"

About two months after the fireplace incident, having finished Alberto's book, I did it. I actually put it down in black and white and told another human of my experience at the fireplace. An email address in the postscript of Alberto's book invited people to let him know of their experiences. Shortly, I received a response from Linda. "Alberto is in Peru, but why don't you join us in July for the Healing the Light Body School?"

CHAPTER THREE

SALINE VALLEY

June 2006

It was now June. I had still not decided upon the July course, nor had I told anyone else about the fireplace incident. Probably never would. But it was time to head to Saline Valley.

Saline Valley is located between the Owens Valley and Death Valley. It is a good two-hour drive in from the paved road, when one is lucky. The winters can be cold, below freezing, and the summers unforgivable.

The hot springs were a sacred and ceremonial site for the indigenous peoples of this region. Many who travel to these pristine waters continue to respect the sanctity and sacredness of this site. However, until this area came under the jurisdiction of the National Park Service in 1994, the thought of routine law enforcement was a joke. In fact, a week before Charlie Manson was arrested at the Barker ranch in the remote Panamint Mountains, Charlie was seen soaking in the hot springs at Saline.

I arrived at this oasis in the desert where there were no others present. I set up camp near the upper spring and immediately shed my clothes as I proceeded to the gravity-fed shower. The shower is a pipe arising from the ground, fed by the healing waters held beneath this land. The shower offers a panoramic view of the mountains and desert that create this valley. The beauty, the expansiveness, and sense of sacredness were rivaled only by the shower at Esalen.

Later that evening while I was soaking in the springs, two ladies arrived, set up camp, and soon joined me in the silence and stillness of the tubs. They were adorned only with necklaces made from the rattles of a snake. It was not 'til several hours later when a rattlesnake approached the waters in which we soaked that the silence between us was broken. I then learned that years earlier the younger of the two women had been struck by the fangs of a rattlesnake, and now she carried the snake as her medicine.

As the conversation continued into the night, I learned this was their first successful attempt to enter Saline Valley and soak in the sacred waters. I learned the one lived in the mountains of Mendocino on twenty acres without water or electricity. Each considered themselves carriers of the ancient medicine ways. They were healers. They used plants from the forest and stones from the mountains to create health. One was fluent in a dialect of the Andes called Quechuan, the language of the Q'ero healers I had just recently learned about at Esalen.

Coincidence or synchronicity, in the twenty-plus years of coming to Saline Valley, this was the first time that I had run into healers that I was aware of, let alone healers of the Q'ero lineage. The next day I headed to the mountains of the Sierra Nevada, having decided to attend the school in July.

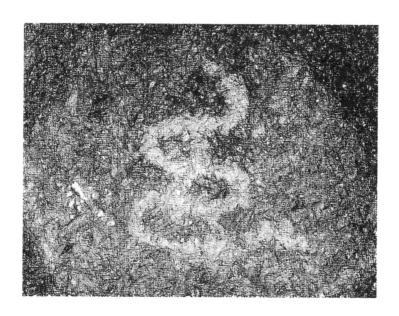

CHAPTER FOUR

THE SOUTH

July 2006

Except for the severe lightning storm north of Cedar City, the drive to Park City, Utah, was unremarkable. I still really wasn't sure why I had decided to come to this class. The email from Linda said, "Why don't you join us in July for a makeup class in our Healing the Light Body School?"

The class information said, "We are pleased to invite you to join the upcoming Healing the Luminous Body School. This is an intensive in energy medicine, following the Inca luminous healing tradition. The Healing the Light Body School is a two-year program leading to proficiency in Luminous Healing. The school was founded by Dr. Alberto Villoldo and is dedicated to training master healers in the practice of energy medicine. The course work includes teaching, hands-on practice, meditation, experiential exercises, and ritual intertwined with personal healing work."

Oh right! I thought sarcastically. *This is the place for me.*

Me, a physician trained in the art and science of Western medicine, a board-certified Family Practitioner, graduate of a well-respected medical school. Me, a member of a professional association whose ethical standards would most likely be breeched should I dare suggest my patients consult with an alternative healer or shaman. *Oh yes! This is the place for me all right,* and yet here I was about to begin a two-year training in shamanic healing.

Spirit had Called Years Earlier

It is said when we call upon Spirit she will always respond. What often is forgotten in our relationship with Spirit is that when Spirit calls, we must respond. Spirit had called years earlier, but I was not prepared for her call, nor did I understand the meaning of her request. I was a father, a husband, a teacher of young doctors and owner of a successful medical practice when Spirit called.

Insidious at first, a strange disorder began to affect my memory and cause my cognition to suffer. Western medicine had been of little help in diagnosing or remedying this situation. Of the earliest diagnoses being offered for my consideration was one of a neurodegenerative disease that granted me a life expectancy of about one year. This was not a diagnosis I wished to entertain or accept. It was however a diagnosis that started a journey. A journey begun more out of desperation than belief. A journey orchestrated by Spirit that has taken me through the realms of alternative healers and their medicine.

It would be many years before I could or would realize that through this crisis of health, Spirit had spoken and changed my destiny; I had been asked by Spirit to leave the practice of medicine to become a healer.

The South Begins

The first three days of this class entailed working with sand paintings, stones, and mythic writings based on the archetypal images of the Tarot. It was the morning of the third day that I realized this was not for me. For some reason, rather than just leaving when class was over at noon, I went up to Linda and asked if we could talk. She told me, not now, but this afternoon. Expecting to talk in private at the first break, I said okay. The afternoon session began, and Linda looked at me "Jim, there is something you wish to talk about..." I looked at the door, looked back at Linda, and then said yes.

We had been working with three aspects, three woundings, of our self to heal. Two of the three woundings I had chosen were trust and vulnerability. Now, as I sat in front of a class of a hundred individuals, the synchronicity of the moment was laughable. I found myself confronting the issues of trust and vulnerability as I discussed my feelings, my experiences, and as I read out loud to the class the mythic story I had written that morning. A story I vowed would never be seen or heard by another.

My words spoken, my soul bare, Linda calmly said the seven words that changed my life: "I am going to do an illumination." Then, she instructed me to blow the essence of my feelings, my emotions, into a stone. Next, she instructed me to lie down on the massage table . . . I did.

As I lay in front of the class, Linda opened an energetic field around me. She called this field of energy the *wiracocha*. In the Quechuan dialect wiracocha means "the Source of the Sacred." It is within this sacred field of energy that healing may manifest.

She then placed the stone, into which I had blown my essence, over my lower abdomen atop my second chakra. This is where she had discovered the blockage. The chakras are organs of the energy body. Blockage or imbalance in these organs may create illness or disharmony in life. As she placed the stone over the second chakra, I heard her say to someone in the class, "Oh, you saw that too!"

At times as Linda was working on me, I felt myself rising above my body, then gently guided back into my form. I was safe, secure, wrapped in a white cocoon of light. I was told to breathe. My breath was deep and involuntary. Then I no longer wanted to breathe. I no longer needed to breathe. I would forever be fine without breath, but I was told to breathe, and I breathed.

I became aware of my second chakra being filled with light and my eyes dashing upwards, then downwards, as if manifesting vertical nystagmus. There was a crystal that appeared between my eyes and then embedded deeply into my forehead. Perhaps it was an hour later or perhaps a minute later, it did not matter, I was back. I had returned. But it was not the "me" who left that returned, for the one who returned was no longer fearful of vulnerability. It was one who could trust.

After the illumination, chilled to the bone, teeth rattling, I step outside to be warmed by the sun. My eyes closed, my body held by the earth, a red owl appeared before me . . . the chills continued. I was not hungry but developed a ravenous urge for meat. Had the spirit of this imaginal red owl come to be fed? I got up to walk to my hotel room. People around me were rushing past me three or four times faster than normal. Each step I took floating, shuffling, like a patient medicated with Thorazine might walk.

As I meandered towards my room, occasionally those who rushed by me would stop to ask if I was all right. Later, safe within the confines of my room, I was startled by the presence of an Aztec warrior. There in full ceremonial dress, just above my left shoulder an Aztec warrior stood behind me. His presence reflected through the filters of a mirror. I did not think to ask or question why.

There Was Smoke

I walked to the elevator, pressed the down button; it arrived on the ground floor, and the door opened. Alberto entered. "Hello, Alfredo!" I said. I didn't make a move to exit . . . He asked if I was going somewhere. "Perhaps," I answered, then stepped from the elevator. In the lobby I saw Marcela. Last time I saw Marcela was at Esalen. I greeted her warmly. *Great, she has no idea who I am.*

Still ravenous for meat, I found everything around me was cleaner, purer, and even colors were more brilliant. I needed quiet and peace. Everything had slowed to half the normal time. I was observing the world from somewhere outside my body. The world was around me, but I was not in it. I was at peace.

That night as we gathered around the fire, Rob approached me. "Man, I need to tell you. When you were on the table in class today, there was smoke coming from your belly, and I thought you were birthing an alien."

The next day, Alberto joined us in class. He would lead us in a journey. We would be journeying to the lower world. I heard Alberto's voice leading us through guided imagery to the lower world. But the landmarks he described were not there. No stream, no meadow in the lower world . . . No, my journey seemed to be going upward into the heavens. I entered a long black vortex, at the end of which there were pulsations of light that beckoned me. As I was pulled deeper into the vortex, shapes and faces appeared.

There was a whitish blue coloration to these forms and faces that took on the appearances of gods and goddesses. As I traveled further into this vortex of energy, it began to open. The skies were dark black and mixed with shades of purple. The colors were transparent, shrouded with a fine white haze as if sheets of lace and satin. The images I perceived were like a three-dimensional photograph that depicted the origin of space, or the birth of a galaxy.

I fought hard not to be drawn fully into the vortex. I knew if I surrendered to this power, I would not return. It was as if I was in water, trying desperately to swim upstream against a strong current that was pulling me deeper into the purple aura of light. I called upon my guides, who I had yet to meet, to be with me. Then traveling upward from the bottom of the vortex, there was a large blue fish. We looked at each other.

I grabbed onto its fin, and clutching it tightly, we began to swim upstream, back into the middle world, the world from which I began this journey. Suddenly I was aware of Alberto's voice saying, "Bring back your power animal even if it has scales and fins." I had not surrendered to the call of the violet aura; perhaps I was not ready that day. I would not have come back.

CHAPTER FIVE

THE WEST

We finished the South. The next step in the medicine wheel will be into the West. The medicine wheel is a map of the journey we walk as we step into our power and wholeness. The South, represented by the serpent, is the shedding of our past. The West, represented by the jaguar, allows us to experience the cycles of death and renewal in life.

I leave Park City and the South unsure if I will return for the West. But I do know that I have to spend the night at Toroweap. Toroweap is on the north rim of the Grand Canyon and is one of the most remote areas of this region. As I turn on to the dirt road, the skies start to darken and cloud. Fifteen miles in, I note a rattlesnake crossing the road before me. I note it because I have never seen a rattlesnake on this road before. The skies continue to darken in front of me, and the smell and feel of fresh rain permeate the air.

Numerous times I just miss the flash flood crossing the road and need to navigate around or through the rocks and brush covering the road ahead. I arrive at the rim, alone. The rain comes harder and the lightning closer. I open sacred space and within moments the skies above me clear—around me the lightning continues to flash, but above me the stars and moon shine.

The next morning, I leave the rim of the canyon, fifty miles out on a different dirt road. I approach an ancient petroglyph site. I start walking down the half-mile trail when I read the sign, "Watch for rattlesnakes." I decide this is not the time; no one knows where I am. Thirty minutes later there is a dead rattlesnake in my path . . . I back up. I'm not one to play with rattlesnakes, dead or alive. I realize this is a gift, a sign for me. I cut the rattles off and bring them with me. I thank jaguar. The living rattlesnake on the way into Toroweap, the dead rattlesnake on the way out, these symbolized the completion of the South, and the beginning of the West.

October 2006

Well, I came back. Most of the people I ran into chuckled and said, "We did not think we would ever see you again." If I had known what was to occur, perhaps I would not have returned. I never did call Marcela in Chile to have the intrusive energy removed. Think part of me still didn't believe it was there.

We broke up into groups of six to practice and learn how to remove entities. I was the fifth to have an entity removed. Reentering the room after cleansing the extraction crystals, I looked at Christy and said, "The energy knows you are coming after it."

Christy was the shaman, the one who runs the extraction. The extraction began. At some point I remember choking, and not being able to breathe. I went down. Apparently, over the next forty-five minutes, the group attempted to bring me back to my body. Except for rare remembrances, I was elsewhere and was not returning. Deborah, the lead teacher, was called over, and as she attempted to bring me back into my body, I remember being asked what was going on. "I am scared" was the reply, but the voice was not mine.

Then I drifted off again. "Cross his arms over his chest. That will stop the flow of energy." Then laughter, intense rolls on the floor, laughter. Again, back to a different reality. "Jim, look at my eyes. Follow my eyes." The connection between Deborah's and my eyes finally pulled me back. I stayed. Later, we cleaned the extraction crystal. Standing outside, Christy handed me the crystal to say goodbye to what was in me. As I stretched my hands up to the skies, I saw an opening and columns of ancient ones, grayish in color, wearing robes, waiting with profound reverence to receive the entity.

My hand and arm were pulled upward as if to pull me up to the ancient ones. I turned to Christy as she said to me, "Yes, I saw it too." She took the crystal and allowed the entity to return home. It was scared and asked, "May I come visit with you?" I said, "No, but when it is my time, I will visit you." That night as I slept, he returned and thanked me. He was home and it was wonderful to be with his family again.

CHAPTER SIX

PRELUDE TO THE NORTH

It is not uncommon when working in ceremony or healing sessions for a client to experience the awareness of others being present. This may be the presence of indigenous healers or visions of angelic forms. Some have witnessed the appearance of their loved ones who have passed before them, and even the appearance of their future healed selves. These are the angels, the bodhisattva, the lineages of healers past, present, and future who have come to assist and to bring health and wholeness for the healing of these individuals.

My awareness of and reconnection to the ancient lineage began a few months prior to beginning the North direction of the medicine wheel. It was the first time I had done a solo fire. The wood and kindling were wet. After trying for thirty minutes unsuccessfully to start the fire, I thought of the "pray rain, be rain story" Alberto had told. A story of a village praying for rain that never came.

Each morning the people of this village looked to the skies and saw the rains falling over a distant village. Envious of what they did not have, they prayed each day for what they lacked and for the gods to rid them of their scarcity. One evening a visitor from these distant lands appeared and sought bedding for the night. As was his custom before retiring, he gave thanks for what he had received that day. He expressed gratitude to the elements of nature—the wind, the sun, the stars, the mountains, and the waters—for the nourishment they had brought forth to the lands.

That night as the visitor slept, the parched lands of this village were quenched by life-giving rains, and the crops that had withered began to flourish. When he awakened, the villagers beseeched him to share the prayers that had brought forth the rains, remedied the drought, and overnight banished scarcity from their village. The visitor replied, "I did not pray to end scarcity. I did not pray for rain. I gave thanks for what I had. I experienced the bounty of the rain. It rained."

I understood. I understood that when we are *trying to be* or *trying to obtain* what we are not or what we do not have in our life, we create an illusion or barrier that separates, that prevents us from being. When we are, we release the illusion of separation. What we desire has not been passed by, nor is it somewhere out in the future waiting, trying to manifest. It is here now. Rain appeared.

I stopped praying, stopped trying for fire. I instead gave thanks to the spirits of the wood and of the kindling. I gave thanks to the air and to the spirits of the fire. I saw the flickering of flames and the fire burning. I gave thanks to the spirits of fire, for the warmth and light it shared with me. I had stopped praying for fire. I had stopped trying for fire. Within seconds fire appeared.

As I sat by my solo fire that night, I knew that I was not alone in this ritual. I knew that shamans around the world were participating in fire ceremony that night. While they sat beneath the stars, warmed by the fires in this ritual of gratitude, they might be sitting alone, in community, or with the spirits and ancestors of the land. I imagined they would be offering thanks for the cycles of life, to the earth, to the moon, to their ancestors, and to all that is.

I was entranced in thought and in the experience as I gazed into the flames. Then I realized that I was not alone. There, sitting on dark, rocky ground and soil not five feet from me, was another. This man wore a red poncho and a colorful beaded hat. I now know it was the same as the indigenous healers wear in Peru. He was sitting in a mountainous terrain that was completely different from my geographic location, yet it was as clear as if I were there.

We watched each other for a while. Occasionally he got up and walked around his side of the fire, and finally I asked who he was. He told me his name was Matthew. A while later I asked where he was. He told me a mountain east of Machu Picchu. We talked a bit, and I asked him what year it was. He responded it was the fifteenth century. He informed me that he was available to me as I needed. Afterward I searched the Internet for Matthew, fifteenth century, found nothing, but realized the Spanish would be Mateo. So next time he appeared, I addressed him as Don Mateo to show respect. He corrected me and asked to be referred to only as Matthew.

Since this first encounter, Matthew has become a constant companion at fires, in ceremonies, with the healing of clients, and as a guide for my own healing.

CHAPTER SEVEN

THE NORTH

March 2007

The North direction of the medicine wheel is about reawakening to who we are. We remember the purpose of our soul's journey. The North is where we become the author of our own story. We become the mythmaker of our creation. In the North we take responsibility for the creation of our world and the course of our life.

In the North, we reconnect with our ancestors and take our seat with the lineage of the medicine men and women who have gone before and will come after us. It is a time of growth, of nourishment, and evolution of our soul. We connect to the sweet nectar of life. We source once again from that which feeds the soul. It is the sense of joy and beauty as we breathe in the sweet fragrances of the rose. It is the smile that arises spontaneously as we glimpse the hummingbird feeding from the flowers.

We speak of the healers of the past and the future. It is of note that we, too, are the medicine men and women of the future and the past. We are available to bring healing and to share our wisdom with the ancient ones who have called into their future for assistance. We are also here to offer our wisdom to the voices of the future that may call to us for guidance.

A few years back, as I worked with my *mesa*, a collection of sacred items and stones, I became aware of a calling, a voice asking for help with a child in an ancient village hundreds or perhaps thousands of years ago. I listened and was aware that the voice was describing the signs and symptoms of a child with an acute appendicitis. Calling upon the experience of my surgical training, I began to visualize this child in surgery, to walk this voice through the steps to remove the appendix. Then I created and offered the image of the child in the healed state to the voice and to the universe. A few days later as I opened my mesa, the voice reemerged, whispering words of gratitude for the miracle of the child's healing.

CHAPTER EIGHT

THE EAST

July 2007

In the East direction of the medicine wheel, we experience death. We work with death. Death becomes an illusion of finality, a moment in the journey of life. Without death, there is no life. Without life, there is no death. We die so that we may live. Death is a point on the circle of our soul's journey. We befriend death. Death becomes our ally.

We call upon death. We ask death, "What must die within, or outside of us, so that we may be born anew?" We step past death into the realms of life. We ask death to take us on the journey of life.

During the death process that which belongs to the earth—the physical body—goes back to the earth; that which belongs to the mountains—the wisdom—goes back to the mountains; and that which belongs to Spirit—the soul—returns to Spirit.

The death rites assist the passage of the soul in the physical form to transition into the next world. When assisting with this transition, the shaman helps the dying soul and their family as they go through the process of recapitulation. This is a chance to hear the client's story, to heal past wounds, and to say *I am sorry* or *I love you*, that which was not said in life.

The process of recapitulation brings closure and forgiveness for the one transitioning. Permission to die is granted. It is said when the last breath has been released, the electromagnetic field dissolves, and the Luminous Energy Field grows into a translucent, egg-shaped torus and takes the seven chakras within. The torus then squeezes through the portal created by its central axis, like a doughnut squeezing through its own hole. This is the eighth chakra. The eighth chakra exists outside of time as the soul, and manifests in time as a matrix for the soul incarnate, the physical body.

For the shaman, death is a transition to life. While the physical body may be relinquished, the soul continues to exist, to grow, and to evolve. We see life as a means of growth and evolution for the soul.

Death allows us to transcend who we are. We have awareness that our perception is only a reflection of our projections. We no longer hold another responsible for the experiences of our life. In the East, we soar with the wings of Spirit. We remember that we are the visionaries, the dreamers, the creators of our world. We remember our connection with Spirit. In the East, we are aware of the new beginnings, the new cycles, that the rising sun brings each morning.

CHAPTER NINE

LIFE AND DEATH IN THE AMAZON

October 2007

Earlier in the summer, I received an email regarding a trip to the Amazon with Marcela. Now a week before the expedition, I again look at the email. What I initially disregarded has become a calling. Phoning the office, I speak with Ruby: Yes, she will speak to Marcela. Yes, they can take one more. Not only that, she then says, "Alberto is on the phone and encourages you to go." I am looking at airfare when my wife calls. "Yes, why not? You are restless." The flight I need and the connecting flights are available. The phone rings; the only appointment I needed to cancel calls me to cancel.

The next afternoon I receive my yellow fever inoculations. I arrive at the airport two hours early. As I wait for the plane to board, I scan the crowd but see no one of interest. The flight boards. I look up from my seat and watch one of the last to step onto the plane; it is Don Francisco. Had I not changed my seat, I would have been just four or five seats from him, but now I am about twenty rows. An hour into the flight, I notice Don Francisco is walking down the opposite aisle. He is dressed in his tan poncho and colorful knitted hat. He looks over and smiles—one of those smiles that shows definite recognition. After he exits the restroom, Don Francisco walks to my seat, and with a deep hug we greet each other warmly.

Don Francisco is a leader of the Q'ero nation. I met Don Francisco six months earlier at a workshop in the desert of Southern California. He had transmitted the nine rites of the *munay-ki* into my luminous body. The nine rites of the munay-ki are a series of blessings and transmissions that raise the vibration of our energetic field. The munay-ki allows us to heal and transform our energy field into that of "homo luminous." This is the light body that the ancient prophecies speak of that will be the matrix of our new being.

At breakfast one morning, Don Francisco and I had sat together and talked. We connected in the manner that only two people who did not speak the same language could, yet we knew exactly what the other meant. Here at 30,000 feet we again communicate similarly. The Chinese man in the seat next to me speaks no English or Spanish but offers up his seat. For twenty minutes, I tell Don Francisco of my trip to the Amazon to meet Marcela, to partake in the ayahuasca ceremony.

I give him my card and he gives me his cell phone number for Cusco. He must return to his seat. Later our path crosses momentarily in customs. He goes ahead and is waiting, but I am held back, and by the time I have finally cleared and retrieved my baggage, he has left.

I arrive in Puerto Maldonado the next morning, have lunch, and take a two-hour motorized canoe trip down the Madre de Dios River to the lodge. That afternoon we meet with Marcela and Panduro. Panduro is the *ayahuascero*. As we will partake of ayahuasca, tonight there will be no dinner. Panduro tells us that he was called to the jungle when he was thirteen years old. He spent three years studying alone with the spirits of the jungle. We are asked, "Why are you here? What do you seek?"

I answer, "The journey. I want to receive all that the spirit of ayahuasca will teach me."

That evening after grabbing our blankets and our mesas, we enter the canoe. This time it is pitch black on the river save for a small flashlight to guide us across. The stars are not visible due to the smoke, and the moon has not yet risen. On the beach we form a circle, the fourteen of us with Panduro in the middle. As we spread our blankets and call on the four directions, he begins to call on the spirits of the sacred land and prepares the ayahuasca. I am one of the last to receive the thick brown sludge that we drink.

When he approaches he looks at me and pours three ounces from a plastic milk bottle into a cup. "Salude," he says. I down this thick brown liquid, realizing as I do, if I stop to breathe or think, I will immediately vomit it back up. He smiles and moves on.

I have heard of the vomiting and occasional diarrhea that accompanies the ceremony, but I know this will not happen to me. So, I sit, warmed by the blanket, and just meditate. Perhaps fifteen minutes later he offers me a smoke from his pipe. It is jungle tobacco. It is strong and acrid. Thirty minutes have passed. From across the circle I hear the first retching, then another poor soul and another. Then it is my turn. I am shocked by the intensity of the first wave. I have just enough time to move five feet from my blanket when the projectile vomiting begins.

I find myself on my hands and knees, retching from the deepest parts of my body. As I stare into the vomit on the sand, there is a pitch-black jaguar staring back at me, its eyes yellow and penetrating. I vomit again. The vomit has to be coming from the lower intestine. I am like a cat whose entire body mobilizes to retch up a fur ball.

I stare at this face of the jaguar in the sand. The jaguar stares back, the eyes so yellow and intense. I feel better now and move back to the blanket. Soon I notice yellow and orange lights darting back and forth through the circle like fireflies. My clothes become so heavy, so constraining, eventually I rip them off. The vomiting starts again. This is only the second wave. The vomiting will continue for the next five hours. In the background I hear Panduro singing and chanting, calling on the spirits of ayahuasca, of the jungle, and on his spiritual assistants to come and heal those present tonight.

The actual sequence to follow is mixed and not ordered, but it is true to the essence. The moon is bright orange, on a roller-coaster track. It dips toward me and back, faster, slower, darting side to side: this will be a recurring scene tonight. I am oblivious to the others. The only connections that exist are with Panduro and the world of ayahuasca that I am in. I am soon to learn that there are many things worse than death. There are the demons we carry within us. There is Beelzebub, the devil.

I am overwhelmed by these visions, by their presence. I lie naked in the sand. Like an animal I begin again to retch. Now the urge to shit comes over me. For what seems like hours, I fight the urge to succumb to the diarrhea, but now the vomiting is so intense, I know if I don't let it out, I will be vomiting shit through my mouth. I get up, now perhaps ten feet farther out of the circle, and I squat. It flows out not once or twice but continually. I have resisted as long as I could; then, when I surrender to the flow, I learn my first lesson.

When I no longer resist, when I release my resistance with honor to the universe, what I have held on to, my beliefs, my judgments, my myths of what should be, they are not as fierce as I have created and held them to be. When I surrender to the flow of the universe, I flow with the power of the universe. Soon I am pacing, chanting. I feel a Native American chief arise from within me, yet I know this is not the one I saw that night in the South, or who has allowed me to chant the ancient songs. I feel Panduro trying to rid me of this entity.

I think back to that afternoon in Park City: while Kelley and I were in ceremony, a Native American chief had come to me and rested upon my energetic body. Is this the energy I am now experiencing? Had I accepted this soul into my energetic field? He is sly, a trickster, and won't easily be taken from my body. He fights Panduro's attempts to remove him.

He survives the smoke blown into my chakras, my luminous field. Across the circle Panduro sneaks up on him, and yes, perhaps he has finally been taken. I am not sure. He has left his wisdom, but he is gone. It was extracted. But the demons remain, taunting me. Panduro is standing over me, blowing smoke from his pipe into my face. The demons continue to come forward, to be seen.

I have no skin, just bones. The ancient ones take me to the fifth world, where I meet Spirit, my celestial parents, and the archangels. They tell me it is time to stay, here in the fifth world, in the crystal city. Negotiating, I say no, I am not finished in this realm. I must go back. We agree for now, but after this life, my place will be in the fifth realm. This is the realm of angels and archangels, of bodhisattvas, of the original self and of Spirit.

I am told about life. Life is a game. Life, our very existence in this physical plane is a game. A game we have chosen to play. A game we play against ourselves. In the game, there is no winner. There never will be. There cannot be. The only way to win the game is to not play. This all makes such sense to me.

There are rules to this game. We must allow the dark to exist if there is to be light. We must let evil exist if there is to be good. The hideous must exist if there is to be beauty. Each is a manifestation of Spirit. Spirit is experiencing itself. If we cage them or try to eliminate them, they will be fierce. But in the game, we can build an altar, and honor them as manifestations of Spirit. For, if we reject them, we are rejecting ourselves and rejecting Spirit.

In the game there is no winner; if we kill these aspects of Spirit, then we kill ourselves and kill Spirit. Let us honor them. Let us honor the vomit and the lakes of diarrhea left in the sand. Let us honor and thank Spirit and Pachamama for receiving these gifts, for digesting them and returning their energy to us.

I lie naked in a fetal position, ten feet out of the circle. I am in the womb. I am being reborn. My soul is being called back, yet there is a strong pull to stay. There is this entity which is attempting to keep me; it is not gone yet. It is not time to return to the ordinary world. There is more to learn, to see, and to experience in the non-ordinary world. The lineage wants me to stay in the crystal city, but I must return and finish this life's purpose. What is this life's purpose?

I am in Death Valley, Saline Valley, perhaps 200 years ago. There are several stranded souls who are being set free and assisted back to the realm of their ancestors, but there is a sheriff, a marshal standing guard over one soul who remains. It is not until this soul has been set free and assisted back to the realm of its ancestors that the soul of the sheriff can be freed to return home. Only then can the energy of my soul be recovered from this site where it has been held for hundreds of years.

The Native American chief is extracted, he leaves his wisdom and knowledge within me, but he is gone from my body.

As I lie in the darkness of the night, rays of golden light flood the beach before me. These rays of light herald the dawn of a new day and a new beginning that offers a new consciousness and a new way of being.

I have met death tonight. Consciously crossed the rainbow bridge and returned. I realize this experience is in preparation for the final crossing, the final death from which we will never again reincarnate. To achieve this final death, we must be awake; we must be seeing and sensing. We must die consciously. We cannot make this final crossing unconsciously. When one enters the next realm to greet the light, it is as a rebirth, a new beginning that must be accomplished in full consciousness.

For the first time tonight, I realize I am cold. I am naked, feeling the sand, the ground beneath me. I am no longer in the womb; I am being born. I begin touching my body, my bones. Symbolically I put on my clothes, patting each inch of myself, feeling my flesh for the first time. Soon my body has been re-fleshed. I am again in human form, back to this world, this reality. I think.

Someone says it is time to go back to the canoe. I walk a few steps. I am exhausted physically, emotionally. I sit down and sleep. I get up again and walk again a few feet, sit down and sleep. This is repeated till I finally reach the canoe. Nancy collapses at my feet in the water on the bottom of the canoe. She announces she is dying. Halfway across the Madre de Dios River, I realize this must be the river Styx we are crossing.

As I climb the steep steps from the river, I begin to fall backward. A force pushes me upright. I look around me. Others look around me. There is no visible being, no one who offered this assistance and yet . . . It is still dark as I awaken to the sound of an orchestra that is composed of the calls of the birds, the monkeys, the animals, and the spirits of the jungle.

Let the Last Breath Be Set free

It begins quickly, but the effects are mild tonight. I have asked tonight to let any work that was not completed from the first night be done, but in the background. Tonight, the focus will be to find my destiny.

There is still retching, still diarrhea, but she is gentle tonight. A portal has been opened for healing. Thousands and thousands of souls have come forth to me to be healed; and then to be guided through the man-made illusion between life and death. It is the work of a shaman to guide the souls who might be lost into the realms of their ancestors.

Jemela's father, George, appears. He has already crossed over, but he is here to heal an issue for his next incarnation.

There is an image tonight, an oil painting of an indigenous medicine man, a wolf, and a hawk on the side of the mountain. They are assisting the souls of the departed to be set free. It is night. They are illuminated by the light of the full moon. There are shades of gray, black, and dark blues. This image persists through the night.

There is also a song that is sung. A song that sings the story of the last soul standing. This song, I am told, refers to the biblical story of Lazarus. As this song is sung, the souls of the land continue to stream forward until the last one has been set free from the earthly realms. Now it is only Lazarus. Lazarus, the wretched old soul, is the last soul standing. He is now free and in that moment I, too, have been freed to continue my journey.

Is my destiny to guide the dying through the illusion of death?

In the Hearts of Man

Tonight, once again Beelzebub appears in my awareness. Just as we honor all aspects of Spirit and of our shadow, one must love and honor him. Perceived in fear and as evil, I build an altar to honor him as a manifestation of Spirit. He is now quieted and at peace with all beings. Regarding love, I am love. I need just to be myself and allow myself to give and to receive love, to be love.

For the shaman, there is no supernatural heaven. There is no hell. For the shaman, there is no independent principle of evil in the universe. Evil is found only in the hearts of man.

This is a world that is composed of the visible and the invisible realms. There exists only that which is and that which is not. A world that exists outside of time, yet within time. This is a world in which the past, the present, and the future are not distinct from one another. It is a world in which all that is and is not is one. It is here in this world that Spirit exists.

The lyrics of *Crystal Blue Persuasion* echoed hauntingly through my head as I began to return to the familiar realms of the middle world. I wish now that I had written down the lyrics as they were sung by the voices of the jungle that night. The voices that sang of a promise for peace and the dawning of a new day. The same voices that raised the frequency of my being and revealed the birthing of verdant new life, rich and abundant in possibility. Nothing like I just heard today as *Crystal Blue Persuasion* played over the radio.

The Sky Is Clear Tonight

The sky is clear tonight. The beach is directly beneath the Milky Way. I watch as star nations and galaxies fight amongst each other. Battles rage between spaceships. There is much activity tonight. War and conflict. Why does there have to be conflict? The ones who are alike will always come together, yet within a group there will always be strife and conflict. It goes back to the game.

God and Spirit, the Creator, are different. God and gods are man-appointed and can be removed. Creator exists outside of time and space and just is. We are all part and representations of the Creator.

Cassanova, our donkey, is of the lineage that brought Mary into Bethlehem from Nazareth. This is the reason why Cassanova will be led but will not pull a cart. It is an honorable lineage.

There is a spacecraft hovering above, and out drops a being that enters and changes the firmware, updates the software, major changes. I do not believe the being leaves, but actually stays and now is guiding from within. The being is now in control of a different type of craft, setting a course for a new journey.

The crystal city, I visit again tonight. At this time, what I learn is elusive. I ask to have recall of what needs to be remembered, to allow the energetic shifts and the healing to occur without need to recall. Despite now trying to change my request, my wish has been sustained. There is much activity in the skies, the galaxies tonight.

As I prepare to leave the Amazon, Panduro suggests I stay and study with him and the spirits of ayahuasca and the jungle. He refers to me as his brother of old.

PART TWO

OF INTEGRATION AND UNDERSTANDING

YEARS LATER

Years Later

It has been several years since I attended the late winter conference on shamanism, a weekend that started me on a journey of consciousness and of awareness. A journey that has taken me back to remote villages in the Andes and into the heart of the Amazon. A journey that has allowed me to explore the ordinary and non-ordinary realities in which we live.

A journey that has welcomed me back to the realm of the medicine men and women of the visible and invisible worlds. A journey that has opened me to the consciousness and spirits of the stones, the plants, the animals, the elements of creation and of all that is. Perhaps this might be a good time to explain the path that I am walking.

It is a path to healing, to wholeness, to health, and to balance. It is a path on which I was again awakened to the cosmovision of the Andes. It is a path on which I was reintroduced to the shamans of the Andes and to shamanism.

CHAPTER ONE

SHAMANS AND SHAMANISM

Shamanism is an ancient tradition of healing and spirituality. The practice and beliefs of shamanism have existed since before the appearance of recorded time and have existed in all regions of the globe.

Shamans are the priests and priestesses of old. They are the men and women who have been called healers by some and known as sages by others. They have access to the wisdom of the universe, and they are the keepers of the ancient knowledge and sacred ways.

Shaman is a description generally applied to healers of indigenous origin by Western cultures. Initially this term was used to refer to the medicine men and women of Siberia. In the Andes and in the jungles of South America, while the Westernized terminology of shaman is generally accepted, the terms *paqo*, *curandero*, or *ayahuascero* will more often be used and spoken by the indigenous communities when referring to these medicine men and women.

A shaman is in service to all of creation, not just those in human form. Through ceremony shamans bring honor and harmony to the worlds of our being. They are the ones who offer thanks to the spirits of the mountains, the waters, and of all that is and all that has been. They are the voices and emissaries between the worlds of creation.

An individual may be called to the path of shamanism through the experience of death or near death. For others it is through a knowing that they must answer and respond to the call they hear from a higher power. In the Andes the initiatory call frequently occurs as one is struck by lightning and survives the event. We in the West may experience this lightning strike metaphorically as our life is turned upside or shattered by an event we hold as catastrophic.

A shaman is often seen as a healer, held as a healer, defined as a healer. Healing is often attributed to a shaman, yet the shaman is not a healer. A shaman helps to create and hold a space in which healing may occur. A shaman is a facilitator of transformation, of transmutation, and of transcendence. Transcendence and transformation allow one to bring forth and source from the unmanifested energy of creation.

This is energy that is devoid of story, judgment, belief, or myth. Energy that allows one to connect to the healer within themselves to create a new way of being. A shaman may facilitate the creation of a bridge between a reality that no longer serves an individual and a reality that empowers and reconnects this same individual to joy, beauty, wholeness, health, love, and light.

Shamans know illness, disease, and turmoil occur when our life is out of balance. The symptoms of these conditions when they are present may be the result of an event or imbalance in life that occurred years earlier. If the origin of the symptoms is not dealt with, then the symptoms may disappear temporarily, but they will continue to reappear until healing of the original wounding occurs.

The universe desires to support our journey to health and wholeness and will continue to find new ways to create opportunities for the wound to be seen and then healed. It is up to us as individuals then to see illness and misfortune not as the creation of an evil universe or vengeful god, but as a benign parent who is helping empower us to heal our past wounds.

In the process of healing, there may be periods of doubt or of discomfort arising as we address the issues of life that we have held as our truth and reality. During these periods we are invited to examine and evaluate the circumstances of our life. Doubt and uncertainty allow us an opportunity to review our current state of being that we may know and experience true harmony, joy, and balance. It is from this place of knowing harmony, joy, and balance that we experience true healing in life.

A shaman works with, yet outside of, our personal myths and stories to shift the energy and change the matrix of the energetic field that informs us. A shaman is one who can move between the illusions of the worlds we have created and the world we desire. These are the worlds of our current reality, our subconscious, and our destiny.

As the shaman accesses these worlds, the cause of disease or turmoil and the path to wholeness may be identified and brought into awareness. The appearance of illness in our life may be an attempt by the universe to heal a karmic event of our past. The appearance of turmoil may be the voice of a past life that desires to be heard and released, or what we see as misfortune may be the basis of our soul's journey to growth and evolution.

Shamanic healing occurs first at the level of the soul and in the energetic matrix of the body. Healing of the emotional and physical levels follows. Healing may occur before the signs or symptoms of disease have manifested in the physical or emotional body. While the healed state may or may not prolong life or cure an illness, it allows for healing and forgiveness, placing the individual in harmony with self, their community, and the universe.

CHAPTER TWO

MAPS

In life, we each have a map and a compass that guides us. The compass orients us to this inner map. This is the map of our life's journey. When the map and the compass are true, we are oriented. We have awareness of who we are, where we have been, and where we are going. These maps are only as expansive and empowering as the cartographer who envisioned the map. We are that cartographer. We have created and drawn these maps based on the influences of our life. When life is in harmony and supportive, these maps serve us well. When life is in turmoil, it may be that the maps we live by are limiting and disruptive to our health and wholeness.

A shaman can help us to discover the influences that have led us away from health and wholeness. A shaman does not collude with the physical or psychological diagnosis with which we present. Our map may present with a diagnosis of cancer, but a shaman does not define us as a cancer patient. A shaman does not treat cancer. He treats the imprint of the cancer along with the fear, anger, and beliefs surrounding the diagnosis. A shaman wishes to discover the map that we have created and that we follow so that a new map, a map of expansive vision and empowerment, may be created.

To heal, we must program our inner compass with new maps that will guide us to our desired destination. The creation of these new maps and recalibration of our inner compass require awareness of the myths and stories that have led us astray. This process of recalibration may occur as we journey through alternate realms of existence guided by a shaman or through the portals provided by the medicine of the sacred plants. Once the influences that have created the faulty maps have been brought into awareness, we may recalibrate our inner compass and begin to draw new maps—maps that we will download into our internal compass to guide us through new lands and into new ways of being.

A shaman transforms the beliefs of what it means to us to have an illness. He works with what was going on in our life years before the onset of the illness or turmoil. A shaman helps to create a new map, a map of wholeness and health. A map that will guide us on this sacred journey we call life.

A map of expansive vision is important because when we limit our vision, our outcomes become limited and our journey incomplete. I had a client I was working with as she sat in an airport lounge waiting to fly standby on the next plane. She had a meeting in another city that required her to be on this plane. As we worked, she envisioned her desire to be on that plane. She abruptly ended our session when she was called to board and to take her seat on the plane. A few minutes later, my phone rang.

She had boarded the plane only to be removed as the original passenger claimed the seat. This individual had successfully manifested herself taking a seat on the plane. She had not envisioned or manifested herself being at the meeting.

CHAPTER THREE

THE ANDEAN COSMOVISION

The essence of the Andean Cosmovision, as I have experienced it, is that we exist in and as part of a benign and supportive universe. All that exists, all of creation, is alive with consciousness and has spirit. All is interconnected as woven threads of a living web of energy through which the flow of this energy and of this consciousness is alive and can converse. It is a universe in which the being of one affects the energy of all and in which the energy of all affects the being of one.

The Andean spiritual path is experiential. There is no right or wrong interpretation of this journey, only perhaps by others who attempt to interpret the journey of another through their own lens. We can be a bridge for an individual on this path, but we cannot walk or experience their journey. We cannot interpret their journey, but we can assist them in finding and shifting their reality if they desire. The experiences and interpretation of this journey are unique for each individual.

During this journey one may experience and be informed by the spirits of the land, the mountains, the winds, and the rivers; or by the spirits of our ancestors or their children, who have yet to manifest in this reality. One must be present and open to the moment, and then allow the experiences and the journey to unfold without judgment or need for interpretation.

The Andean Cosmovision engages the world on four levels, defined as the physical, the mental/emotional, the mythic, and the energetic. To experience this journey, one must allow one's spirit to engage reality from the level of the mythic and the energetic. Levels that we in Western society might not be comfortable in or even acknowledge that they exist.

Our reality is interpreted by our mind, based on the lens of our beliefs, experiences, and myths. It is also based on the beliefs, experiences, and myths of our families, cultures, and societies. Trance states allow us to view reality without the interpretation of the mind, whether induced through meditation, chanting, rattles, or plants (entheogens). We stay out of the mind and then we can be present for the experience. One must let go of the need to understand the journey. Understanding may reveal itself later, or not.

Ayni

Illness of a physical, mental/emotional, or spiritual nature is believed to be caused when one is out of right relationship with self, community, or Spirit. This is the concept of *ayni*. To be whole, to be in health one must be in ayni. When one is out of balance, one is out of ayni.

Ayni is balance. Ayni is being of service and in right relationship with the cosmos, with our community, and on an individual level with our self. It is a supportive, loving relationship between all that exists, between all that is.

Ayni is sacred reciprocity. We give, we receive. We receive, we give. We give what we can, and in return the receiver gives what they can, when they can, and to whom they can. Hence, when I give, then I receive, and when I receive, then I give.

Ayni is not a payment for goods or services; it is an acknowledgment, a thank-you. It is an act of gratitude for what has been done or what might be done in the future.

Ayni occurs not only between humans but between all of creation. Sacred reciprocity exists between the llama and the shepherd, between Mother Earth, the farmer, and the harvest. The shepherd watches over the llamas, protects them from predators, and brings them to fresh pasture. In return the llama produces wool to weave and dung to cook with. The llamas carry the harvest and goods up and down the mountains of the Andes.

Each year the llamas are honored in ceremony for their service. Pachamama produces beautiful corn. In return the best corn is returned to Pachamama, thanking her for her abundant harvest. The mountains, clouds, and wind receive thanks for the rain they bring, and for keeping away the hail and the lightning that might devastate the crops.

Ayni is the place of *munay*, the place of unconditional love. It is not the human love of romance. It is the love of the flowers and seeds for the life-bringing rain or the warmth of the soil in which the seeds germinate. It is the love of honoring our enemies as fellow human beings. It is the love of compassion and of forgiveness, both for ourselves and for others.

When our thoughts, heart, and actions are in alignment, we are in balance, we are in integrity, we are in ayni. Illness, turmoil, and disease occur when we are out of balance, out of integrity, out of ayni. Let us take a moment to look at our life through the filters of ayni: Where might our life be imbalanced? Are we in integrity with our thoughts, our heart, and our actions? Are our actions saying one thing, while our heart and beliefs tell us something else?

Our Salka Being

Salka is our natural state of being, our undomesticated self. Salka is our essence, disrobed of the clothing of society and culture. In the West, we have forgotten our salka self, our essence. We have forgotten our individual truths, as we give way to the truths of family, of society, and of our culture. Western culture and society emphasize and value the domesticated way of being based upon the myths of Western society. As Western domesticated beings, we forget who we are in the greater cosmos. It is time once again to remember who we are.

In the West, consciousness is limited to the human realm, to our individual essence or thought. In the Andean Cosmovision all that exists in creation has an individual consciousness, a spirit, and an essence. All that exists also is part of the cosmic consciousness, the energetic web that integrates and reflects all that is and is not. This cosmic consciousness is dynamic. It reflects the energy of all. Whenever the individual shifts, the whole shifts. When the whole shifts, the individual shifts. This is the web of life.

In the web of life, there are threads, like the threads of a tapestry or of the web of a spider. Where these threads cross and come together, there is a confluence of energy that creates a form. This form may be a mountain, a flower, or even a human being. Each form has an individual consciousness that creates the whole. The whole has its own consciousness made up of the consciousness of all. Just as individual dots within a painting create a whole painting, the threads create the tapestry of the universe.

When we release the barriers of the individual forms, we once again remember the consciousness of the whole, of the cosmos. We reconnect with the cosmic consciousness. We are no longer separate from nature and the cosmos. We are nature. We are the cosmos. We are the whole. We remember that we are not separate from Spirit— we *are* Spirit. We are the creator of our world and universe.

Hucha

Hucha is energy. It is heavy, dark energy. Hucha is created by discordance. When we are out of ayni, out of harmony with our self, our community, or with Spirit, we create hucha. It is the energy that spewed from my side as I stood in front of the fireplace. It is energy that by itself does not feed or nourish us. It is not good, nor bad. It just is. We as individuals assign beliefs to this energy or we may interpret its quality. We judge the energy as good or bad.

By these acts of projection, we create a vibratory essence or signature that becomes assigned to this energy that may then be disharmonious to our self or others. When we hold onto this energy that has now been assigned a quality, it can create illness, turmoil, or discord in our life. Yet this is just energy—energy that I may experience as heavy, yet another may experience as light and nourishing. It is all the same energy. It is our perception and our projection of judgment onto this energy that create the quality as heavy or light.

Pachamama, Mother Earth, enjoys eating the heavy energy known as hucha. To Mother Earth this hucha is not heavy and burdensome; this is nourishment. This energy is full of rich nutriments that have been given freely to her. She then transforms what we perceive as heavy energy into *sami*. Sami is the vibratory essence of joy, beauty, love, and light. It is light, refined energy that feeds and nourishes life. Think of the cow that poops in the field. The poop is heavy energy to the cow. To the earth, this poop is full of nutriment-rich energy that once transformed will be a source of sustenance for the flowers. This is an act of reciprocity, of ayni.

We can release heavy energy from our body and energetic field directly to Mother Earth. This heavy energy may be in the form of thoughts, beliefs, or emotions of anger, fear, or shame. This energy may be free-floating within the energetic field or crystalized within the cells of our physical body. First, we ask permission of Mother Earth; next we visualize an energetic connection from our base chakra that anchors deeply into the soils of Mother Earth. Then with intent, we release the heavy energy we carry to her. Simultaneously we visualize a funnel that through the crown chakra creates access to our energetic field. It is through this point of access that the refined energy of sami flows to fill the void created as we release the heavy energy from our body.

This release of hucha to Pachamama is an act of ayni. We nourish Pachamama with our hucha, and she in return feeds us through her offering of sami. This exchange is no different than how in the cycle of life we receive oxygen that is essential for life from the plants, and in return the plants receive from us the carbon dioxide that is essential for photosynthesis and survival of the plant.

Yachay, Munay, Llankay

To be in ayni with self, the Andean Cosmovision recognizes three centers of being. The first center is located at the forehead and is known as *yachay*. Yachay are our thoughts. The second center is located at the heart center and is known as *munay*. Munay is love that is unconditional. Munay is the energy that harmonizes our thoughts and our action to be of service to Spirit and the universe. The third center is located at the belly and is known as *llankay*. Llankay are our actions and our deeds.

When we are in ayni, our thoughts, love, and actions are in alignment. This is manifest in our personal life, as the universe and our community reflect back to us these same qualities to create balance and health in our life, our community, and our relationship with Spirit.

Complementary Opposites

When all is in balance, all is in ayni. There is harmony and abundance. There is wholeness and health. The Cosmovision of the Andes is one that recognizes and honors difference. In fact, this vision acknowledges that without difference, *other* cannot be recognized. It is known day cannot exist without night; man cannot exist without woman; woman cannot exist without man.

Opposites require each other to exist. Without darkness there is no light. Without light there is no darkness. In the Andean Cosmovision, this awareness of complementary opposites is known as yanantin.

There is no judgment; one state of being is not better than the other. One is not in competition with the other—they just are. One state of being is also not separate or distinct from the other. In quantum physics a wave can be a particle, or a particle can be a wave, the distinction being dependent upon one's reference of measurement. In the Andes the characterization of masculine and feminine is relative and dynamic, dependent upon one's reference of measurement. A mountain is most often categorized as masculine when it stands alone; however, this same mountain when compared to another may be characterized as feminine. This dynamic categorization is dependent upon the qualities that define the mountain when in relationship to another. For example, a larger, more jagged mountain would be described as masculine when compared to a mountain that is softer, rounder, and of a more feminine nature.

Duality in Unity, Unity in Duality

Duality in unity, unity in duality. Unity exists as a conglomerate of all that is, and yet within duality there is no whole; there is no unity. It is the complementary properties of duality that, when in balance, allow for creation of a whole yet separate consciousness of being. The yin-yang exists only because of the individual unities of the yin and the yang. Herein lies the concept of duality within unity and unity in duality: the awareness that one state cannot exist separate and independent of its opposite, yet these states cease to exist as whole.

CHAPTER FOUR

THE SHARING OF WISDOM

Long before human beings appeared, the consciousness of the cosmos was alive and omnipresent. Some believe that a breath from the great void of creation brought forth the cosmos. This breath of creation manifested in swirling winds that coalesced into stars or brought forth particles into planets.

There was a cooperation and sharing of wisdom amongst all that was creation. The winds spoke to the sun and the stars, sharing with them the history of their journey. As Earth began to take form, the wind told of the great medicine that the stones held and how they could bring forth fertile ground for the spirits of the plants to take root. The winds also spoke of the great rivers and oceans that would be held by the contours of the stones. The sun, the stars, and the moon were in harmony with the oceans and fertility of the lands. They observed and learned the wisdom of life and shared with one another these mysteries.

As humankind appeared, this wisdom and the attributes of the plants, the stones, and the night skies were shared with the indigenous ones. The stars foretold of the seasons and of the rains. As the constellations cycled through the night skies, they announced the times to plant the seeds and the times to harvest the crops. Nature and creation freely shared their gifts with the indigenous beings of Earth who received this wisdom with gratitude and honored the spirits of these realms with gifts of celebration.

Voices of the Ancient Wisdom

The voices of the plants, the stones, the winds, and nature are the oldest voices of Earth. When we listen to these voices, they provide a means for the ancient wisdom and knowledge of the universe to be shared. We have an opportunity to learn from their wisdom, and to heal our relationships with the universe.

But we, in the Western systems of beliefs, have attempted to separate and isolate ourselves from nature. We have neglected the wealth of wisdom and of teaching that is available from these realms of being. Not so our indigenous brothers and sisters, who remember and still speak with the spirits of these realms. In ceremony they honor, they listen, and they celebrate these sources of knowledge, healing, and wisdom.

It is time for us in the West to remember our connection with these spirits. It is time for us to remember that we are no different than the streams, the stones, the trees, or the llamas that grace the earth. It is time for us to remember that we are the children of the earth, the sun, and the cosmos. We must again respect and celebrate with our mother, the earth, and our star brothers and sisters. When we remember that we are not separate from nature, we will return to ayni with our true essence, our salka self, and our natural state of being. We will be in right relationship with all that is.

The wisdom, knowledge, and ancient memories of the stones and the plants are available to each of us. We need just to listen. The indigenous ones know this fact. When asked about how the healing properties or attributes of plants became known to the early healers, they have answered, "The plants told us."

There are many plants that are known or referred to as master teachers or master healing plants. We, in the West, have the opportunity to access their teaching as well. We must just be available to hear their voices and witness their stories. Through this connection, these plants may provide access to ancient wisdom, create balance and healing, or bring forth answers as to the origin of turmoil within a life.

Plants such as *wachuma* or the tea brewed of ayahuasca and *chacaruna*, when ingested orally, bring us into direct contact with this wisdom and knowledge. Together wachuma and ayahuasca allow us to access the energy of creation. Ayahuasca and wachuma both heal, both teach. They bring us knowledge and awareness of our conscious and unconscious self. They bring awareness to the journey of our soul. If I were to characterize, I would say that ayahuasca allows us to see why we are. Wachuma, in contrast, brings us vision that allows us to see and to remember who we are.

CHAPTER FIVE

AYAHUASCA: MASTER PLANT, TEACHER, AND HEALER

Ayahuasca is one of the master healing plants. Ayahuasca is also a teaching plant. The indigenous ones say we never walk alone. They say our shadow always is with us. The shadow is that part of our being we wish to disown, that part we wish not to acknowledge exists within us.

The shadow carries within it the unconscious influences, beliefs, and myths that we have incorporated into our reality. Ayahuasca brings awareness to our shadow and these unconscious influences. This awareness allows us to act and respond consciously to the events that arise within our life.

The indigenous ones say our future is behind us, that with each step we take, we meet our past. This past that created our stories, beliefs, and judgments of what is to be as we take our next breath. It is this past that has created our future, that has created our present being, this perception of life we call reality. Ayahuasca allows us to understand and to heal our past. It allows us to transform our past as our future moves through our present reality.

This concept that our future is behind us may seem confusing, yet it is quite simple. We create our future expectations based on our past experiences. We live in a world that is linear. A world that is based on the past. I was hurt. I was wronged in the past. I will be hurt and I will be wronged in the future. My future has been created. The past sweeps through me to create my future. Hence the past is my future. The past moves in front of me to create my present moment.

Our future is a learned belief that, without a transcendent intervention to transform our knowing, will remain our reality. We bring forth our vision. We energize this vision of the future. We manifest this vision as our reality. Only in the present can we choose not to allow the past to move before us to create our future reality. When we have awareness, we may choose to transform this energy as it passes through us. Then we have transcended the past and created in the present a reality free of our past experiences and our beliefs of what will be. We create a future (i.e., a present) based on a past that no longer holds us hostage to our beliefs and experiences.

Ayahuasca allows us to heal our trauma, to transform our beliefs. Ayahuasca brings light to our shadow. Ayahuasca allows us to travel back in time to heal the wounding in the present. It is the catalyst of a transcendent event that allows us to see life in a new perspective and with new vision. We heal our past, we change our future, and we change our destiny.

In my experience, Ayahuasca brings light and awareness to the creation of the myths and stories that shape and influence who we are and who we are becoming. Ayahuasca brings the voice and the vision to the issues within our life that may require healing. It allows us to know and understand the events that have created our being, that have influenced why we are this person, this being in life today.

Ayahuasca teaches through creating a stage for us to observe and interact with the energy of the cosmos. We become the main character and the supporting actors on this stage. We are each playing a role we have selected. The universe is the stage, our soul is the director, and ayahuasca is the producer of this play.

Ayahuasca heals by allowing the voice of an event, the voice of an emotion, or the voice of pain to be heard. On this stage, the ghosts and demons of our life and of our own creation are faced, heard, and honored. We are the ghosts; we are the demons.

Once these voices have been heard and acknowledged, these demons and ghosts no longer call for attention. The actors have been honored. Now their energy is transformed and can create new scenes, new players that will serve and empower our life, our being.

The vision ayahuasca brings may present in many forms and through many senses. We may see, we may feel, both physically and emotionally. We may embody the old story, letting it play through us, and us through the story. Once the role and lesson have been voiced and heard, then we can shift how we play the role. Once the story is transformed, we may heal, and we become empowered.

Healing during the journey may come through an extraction of energy that is intrusive. It may come through soul retrieval, through the reintegration of self, or the death of self. It may manifest through the receiving of gifts, of power animals, or through the changing of old contracts that no longer serve us into new empowering contracts and beliefs. These new contracts, supported by new myths of creation, become the basis of a new reality and way of life. Or perhaps the healing occurs just by acknowledging and hearing the story the energy needs to tell.

It is said of the sacred plants that once their medicine works with us, the spirit of these plants will always be with us, available to bring forth healing and to share the wisdom they hold. During ceremony with ayahuasca I have observed many times as the strands of my DNA have unraveled and intertwined with the vines of ayahuasca, creating a double helix composed of my DNA and the DNA of this master plant. This, an embodiment of the wisdom and the healing properties of the medicine, an embodiment of the spirit of ayahuasca.

The Journey at Tubac

Tonight, I am confronted by my ego and by my judgment—judgment that I have created of my own self, and by the judgment I fear that others will hold of me, or I of them. I see my thoughts and my fears, my doubts and my uncertainty manifest immediately. Tonight, I am confronted and challenged by the understandings of trust, humility, and doubt.

As I tried to formulate my intent for ceremony during the week preceding, ego continued to present itself. Yet as ego is apt to do, I refused to see this as what I needed to work with this weekend. I denied and dismissed that this was my journey, my healing for the weekend. I should have known.

It was now my turn to drink and to face my ego. I had not even returned to my seat when the urge to vomit swelled over me. Time after time I forced the contractions and the medicine back down to be held within me. Not wanting to appear as the weak one, the one who could not hold the medicine, I resisted. My ego resisted. I would not be the one to vomit before the forty-five minutes had passed, yet I was so ready. My ego was proud.

Then I vomited. Twenty minutes in I vomited, loud and explosively. I was the first one to vomit that night, the loudest in this room of silence. My fear manifested for all to witness. This fear was based on "ego." I heard the voice of my ego speaking: *How will the others judge me? How do I judge myself?* This fear was based on the ego's fear of judgment.

Yet, herein is the lesson of ego and judgment. When I choose to accept the judgment of another to define me, I give away my power to be who I am. When I no longer define myself, I then become defined by the beliefs and judgments of others. As I view myself as they view me, I begin to accept and live the myth they wish to create of me. The myth of disempowerment or the myth of weakness, "Yes, I am the weak one, the one who could not resist the purge."

Judgment is the act of interpreting an event or situation as good or bad. This judgment is through the lens and eyes of the judge. What might be interpreted as good by one individual may be interpreted as bad by another. What is out of balance or disharmonious for one may in fact be in balance for another. Hence, the filters of the judge create the interpretation and place the quality upon the event. I had given my experience, my healing with the medicine, away to others to judge who I was. In fact, I had given my eyes away to others as I judged myself through the eyes and filters of others.

I resisted the call for the purge based on the truths of others. Yet the spirit of the medicine had been working with me days in advance of tonight's ceremony, so the onset of the purge was perfect when it happened. When we release judgment of what is, what has been, or what may be, all is perfect as it is. We can change, not because we need to change but because we desire to.

Tonight, I was shown the karmic energy of this situation as it was. For it was I who, in another time, judged which souls would enter the kingdom of heaven or be sent to the inferno of hell. I, as Saint Peter, held the keys to heaven. I determined evil and good through my filters, my lens. I judged not only the individual, but I judged the qualities of heaven and hell. Heaven was for the energies of good, and hell was for the energies of evil. It was I who created heaven and hell.

As the teachings progressed through the night, I was shown that the energy I judged as evil and bad through my filters may be harmonious, necessary, and healing for the growth of another. Just as light is necessary for the growth of a sprouted seed, darkness is required for the germination of this same seed. As the teachings continued I learned that it is within darkness that a seed germinates and sprouts, transcends itself as a seed, to become a mighty oak. It is from within the darkness of our life that our soul grows and transcends to a new being. In fact, just as with the seed of an oak tree, darkness may be required as the next step in growth of the soul.

Karma

Semi-naked, drunk, disheveled, dying, pitying myself, begging for mercy, hugging the floor of a public restroom, neglected by those who passed by. Here, I, too, judged my soul's journey as I would beg of those who passed by, those who would judge me, for forgiveness, mercy, and sustenance. Just as I had judged what was harmonious, what was good or evil for each soul, I found others to judge me. Through this act, I learned of humility and to be humbled.

Not seen, alone, and neglected. Then a soul saw me, touched me, and offered me hope. The voice only asked, "Are these your pants?" The voice did not offer to bring the pants to me or to support me as I dressed myself. The voice just asked the question and invited me to put them on when I found the strength within myself to do so.

The voice touched me, brought me awareness. The voice offered hope. Hope not that I would be rescued but that I could find the resolve, the power within me to rise again from the depths to which I had fallen. It would have to be my connection to the healer within me from which I could draw the power to put on my pants and to heal.

Hope yielded possibility, which manifested growth and a return to wholeness. I found throughout the journey that what I thought I had processed mentally about humility, compassion, and munay was just that, done mentally. I did not know humility or compassion at all.

I begged for help, for healing to come. I pleaded for forgiveness. I pleaded for mercy, to release myself from my karma. It was not until I *became* mercy that I *had* mercy. It was not until I forgave myself that I received forgiveness. When we do not forgive another, when we do not forgive ourselves, we hold ourselves in the prison of the past, and of our own anger or hurt around the event.

As I journeyed that night, I embodied this energy at the level of the cells and atoms. What previously were only concepts of the mind were brought into a visceral basis of understanding and knowledge to draw upon. I now knew the power of hope. I now knew humility and compassion. I now understood and experienced the power and nourishment of unconditional love.

We must find love, peace, and tranquility within ourselves. We must be what we desire to receive what we desire. We do not look for comfort, joy, love, beauty, and safety outside of ourselves. Instead, we find these qualities within us. We embody these qualities. Then we are comfort, joy, and beauty. We become peace, love, and light. To heal, we find the healed state within us. When I became mercy, then I had mercy.

The body responds to the beliefs of the mind and the myths of the soul. We create new myths, new beliefs. We create a new reality, a new body, through which to experience and live our reality. The medicine that night empowered me to shift. The medicine was the facilitator to allow myself to "be" and to accomplish whatever I desired.

For healing to occur we must desire the change. We must be the change. We may be blocked as our beliefs that change cannot occur manifest in our reality. There may be secondary gain to stay where we are. We may hold attachment to who we are in illness or turmoil. When we release our attachment to an illness, the power it holds over us flows from us.

For healing to occur we must trust where we are on this journey. Where we appear stuck may be exactly where we need to be to heal, to evolve. Here in the darkness of our growth, we may become aware of what is needed, what is desired, not what we are entitled to from life or from Spirit. Here in the darkness, I stopped looking. As I started seeing my wholeness, I became whole.

The shaman (or spirit of the plant) facilitates the healing process by creating hope and the possibility for change. But the "I" must desire change in order to change. There must be no back doors. There must be no uncertainty that change can occur. Back doors and uncertainty allow fear to manifest and inhibit change.

We manifest with our thoughts. If our thoughts are of fear and doubt, then we will manifest into our life that which we doubt or fear. If we shift our thoughts from doubt to certainty and trust, we will begin to manifest certainty and trust in our life. This manifestation of our thoughts, be they conscious or unconscious, is based upon the universal laws of attraction. These laws theorize that we attract into our life that upon which we focus. Think of the power when we shift our beliefs from "I am not worthy, I cannot do it," to "I am worthy, I can do it, I can be ..." But it is not enough to just change our beliefs. We must also create a new myth to feed the new beliefs, a myth that will anchor the new beliefs into our cells, our physical body, and our soul.

Tubac Continues

Tonight, I drink only a small amount. My intent for tonight is to release myself from scarcity and to source instead from abundance and balance.

I begin to see and to experience a life in which the umbilical cord is wrapped around my neck. I am in utero. The amniotic fluid is thick with meconium. I struggle for breath. I cannot breathe. I die before I am born into life. Although who I was has died, the spirit of this soul still lives in scarcity within me, influencing my beliefs, creating who I am. Tonight this soul is freed, released to its spiritual family. No longer needing to live in scarcity or to struggle, this soul now rests. And I, no longer informed by whom I have been, am free to source from abundance and balance.

As ceremony draws to a close tonight, a single candle is lit in the darkness of the room. From this one point of light, the darkness in which we have been held is illuminated a thousand times.

CHAPTER SIX

WACHUMA: MASTER PLANT, TEACHER, HEALER

My work and my journey with the sacred teachings of wachuma began several years ago at a home in Laguna. The master teacher wachuma, perhaps better known as San Pedro, had been in my awareness and beckoning me for almost a year. The morning of the ceremony, I drove an hour south to the small beachside community of Laguna, where I and twenty others gathered in ceremony with this teacher. I had not understood why I was called to attend this particular ceremony, yet when the invitation was offered, there was no doubt, I would be present.

The journey was facilitated by a shaman from Peru known as La Gringa. La Gringa, South African by birth, was a blonde-haired, blue-eyed woman in her fifties who in the early nineties was called by Spirit to work with the essence of San Pedro and to facilitate and share the opportunity, the teachings, and the experience of wachuma with others who sought this wisdom.

The morning started with a *despacho*. A despacho is a ceremony and an offering of gratitude. We offered our thanks not only for what we had received in the past but also for what we would receive in the future. A web of yarn was created symbolically connecting each of us to this web of life and to a central point, reminding us of our connection to each other, to the universe, and to Spirit. This web connected our intentions and our prayers for the ceremony that day. The powdered San Pedro was mixed with water and quickly drunk as we offered our individual intent and prayers to the spirit of this teacher.

Sometime within the next thirty minutes, a deep, subtle state of relaxation developed. Then, a dreamlike sleep overtook me. During this sleep, the portal through the cosmos opened. There were voices joined together in song and a cacophony of indigenous dialects being spoken yet understood by all. I became aware of the gods and goddesses that were present. There was a stairway between the realms that facilitated their movement.

There was the awareness that we were all one, coming together through the veils and illusions of separation. This was a gathering of spiritual beings, a gathering that occurred every 26,000 years, a gathering where we as healers rested. We had come together for rest, for healing, and for nourishment, to again be reacquainted and share our experiences of being. We had come together to play.

Wachuma is often associated with the healing powers of the hummingbird, whose medicine opens our heart to remember our connection to the cosmos and bathes us in the love and light of Spirit. As the ceremony waxed and waned, there were times of telepathic communications between those present. We were the gods of creation. There were lessons and reminders for the being I call Jim. Lessons that I would remember and integrate into my being as the effect of ceremony passed. These were the reminders of our connection to Mother Earth and to the cosmos.

There were reminders about the power of intent, that intent and visualization manifest outcome and form. There were the reminders that when working with clients, to connect with the spirits of the stones, the feathers, or the rattles as it is the spirits of these beings that bring healing and transformation. There were the reminders that as we call in the mountains and the rivers, the spirits of these energies are working with us, creating healing and balance, sharing their wisdom. There were the reminders to take the time to heal and nourish oneself.

There are hours unaccountable for that day. I had opened my mesa. I was performing the death rites upon our animals, the ones who had passed. When complete, I rested. I lay down to awaken in a meadow surrounded by a lineage of indigenous healers working to release past wounds and to bring healing. I was being healed. A black rain came and began to devour the darkness from the left side of my belly. A bullet was removed from my right shoulder.

There was an extraction of energy, a form that was not mine. Indigenous maidens appeared and bathed me in the essence of flowers and pristine spring waters. I was in a place of deep relaxation, profound tranquility and peace.

Later as I worked with this teacher, I found myself in chaos, bereft. Then there was the voice of an older woman asking, "Why do you hold on to it? What does it mean to you?" I was told I had freedom to choose, to choose who I am, where I am, to let go of how and what I experience as my reality. She said if I do not want to be in a situation, I need not be there. She said if I do not wish to experience pain, to experience fear or anxiety, then I may shift to another experience, another frequency, another focus.

There was an awareness that came to me at that moment. An awareness that I could create my own journey. An understanding that we are the gods who create the myths of our being and the myths of our journey. These may be myths of empowerment or of dependency, myths of joy and beauty, or the myths of victimhood and deficiency. We could choose our journey. We, alone, could choose to create the path to our fate, our destiny. We could choose to be a victim or choose to be the creator of this journey. The choice was ours.

Wachuma allows us to remember who we are. We are the gods. We are the grandfather in the jungle. We are the man in Haight-Ashbury who is trapped in death, dying again and again. We are the one, no longer grounded in body, no longer a participant in a collective reality as we experience the realms of an individual dementia. We are the one writing this story.

Later that year, I am in the hills above Cusco, adjacent to the Temple of the Moon. As Danny, the shaman I am with today, begins to share his wisdom of the Andean beliefs and cosmology, I cannot help but notice that there are bluish green stripes nearly an inch wide running along the length of his cheek and jaws. As he talks, his body has taken on the qualities of a great black jaguar. I am aware of being transported with him into a different realm of being, and we have yet to drink of the medicine.

Soon I begin my journey. I am reminded that munay is the universal language. It is the language of love, that munay is unconditional love. Today this journey is a journey of unconditional love for the universe. I learn of the darkness, and how darkness need not be feared but should be honored. We are born of the void from the darkness. It is the darkness that holds the stars. It is from darkness that life springs forth. That life evolved.

I am once again reminded that "I have choice," choice of my path and of my destiny. To have a choice I must be fully present in the moment. If I am not perfectly in the moment, if I am held by the past or by fear of the future, then I am not present. When I am not present, when I am held hostage by past events, then a response is not a choice; it is a reaction.

It is late afternoon when we approach the entrance to the Temple of the Moon. I step through the mouth of the serpent as I enter the temple. Once within the cave, there are chambers; chambers which Danny describes to me as the chamber of the brain and the chamber of the heart. A narrow passageway leads from the chamber of the brain. I can only step sideways as I pass through this narrow crevice. There is a rush of energy. I step back into the chamber of the heart. I become aware of the presence of the condor and of the wolf on the ceiling of this chamber.

There is an altar of stone. I place my mesa on this altar; then I am called to offer myself to this stone altar. I become ensconced in a golden white light. It is Inti, the Sun God. I am initiated as a child of the light, a child of the sun, a child of the stars. I become this light. As I step from the cave, it is a process of birth, of rebirth.

Danny appears, informs me that I have been reborn as a child of the light. I am a being of light. As I descend from the steps of the temple, I go down upon my knees, and as I kneel, I connect to the brightness of the sun. I am again encased in a cocoon of pure golden white light. The same light I had been held in by Linda during the illumination she had performed that day in the South.

Focus

In life where and how we choose to focus our attention, whether it is on the past, the present, or the future, determines the current state of our beliefs, our truth, and our being. When we choose to focus with the eyes of a human, we create partitions and barriers that prevent us from seeing through the illusions of space and time. These illusions keep us anchored to the wounds of the past and may prevent us from moving forward through limiting beliefs into wholeness and health.

When we shift our focus and view life through the eyes of an eagle soaring high above the plains of ordinary reality, we see that the past, present, and future are all occurring now within the totality of existence. We see the purpose of the adversity we are experiencing in life for the growth of our soul. Through the eyes of hummingbird, we may see our life in wholeness, brought into balance and into right relationship within all the realms of existence available to be lived and experienced.

Past, present, and future, incarnate or reincarnate are all an illusion of time. They are all simultaneous; they are all occurring now. The master teacher wachuma has shown me the existence of these concurrent lifetimes. I have been shown life as it would be if I energized myself as the grandfather in the rain forest or the life where I am confined to an institution with dementia. I have been given a choice by the spirit of wachuma as to which life I return to and focus on in the present, an energized moment that I choose to experience as life.

The Spirit of Wachuma

Many years later, I found myself walking in solitude through the back gardens of a villa in the hills above Los Angeles. I had asked to know the spirit of this teacher, to understand the medicine and the spirit of this cactus. I had asked to know, to understand wachuma, to meet the grandfathers, the spirits of San Pedro. As I walked, I was drawn to a tree swarming with hummingbirds. At first, I watched from a distance as the hummingbirds danced and fed from the multiple feeders and flowers.

At some point I became aware of a woman as she sat beneath this tree, communing, speaking with the hummingbirds. I stood quietly, so not to disturb this sacred moment. Then she turned and invited me to share this sacred space, this sacred moment, outside of time with her.

For hours I sat beneath this tree watching the hummingbirds come and go. At times their iridescent bodies hovered so close to me that I would feel the vibration of their wings as they brushed so gently against my face. They were here to heal, to share their medicine with me, with us.

From time to time others participating in ceremony appeared. As they sat beneath this tree, they would release their tears, their fears and frustrations to Mother Earth, and then move on. Soon it would be my turn.

I was in a trancelike state when suddenly I became aware of a rattle that had manifested in my hand. A rattle engraved with the image of a hummingbird. Then just as suddenly, I felt the impending urge to vomit—an urge that rose from deep within the cells of my body and soul. Yet all that was released to Mother Earth as I vomited were the sounds of anger, sorrow, and anguish, all from ancient times, ancient lives, and ancient beings.

There were two souls holding space, a man and a woman in balance, in support of one another, in support of me. She was the priestess of this temple, the source of love and light, the nectar that fed and nourished the hummingbirds; and he provided the grounding for her medicine.

I felt the compassion, the support, and the wonderment of others who came to witness and honor the experience of my healing. Their presence allowed the trauma and stories held within me to surface and to be released. A release of energy that was deep, ancient, and unworldly in nature.

I returned to this tree two years later and I asked once again to know, to understand the grandfathers of wachuma. When I first asked this question two years earlier, I received love, joy, beauty, compassion, and bliss. This time I was joy. I was love. I was compassion. I was beauty. I was bliss. I understood. I knew wachuma. The spirit of wachuma had embodied me with its gifts.

I know who wachuma is. I know this in gratitude.

Chapter Seven

Stones

Stones are historians. They bring us knowledge of ancient times and events. They are the witnesses to time, and they are the voices for the events prior to the appearance of plants or man.

Stones appear in many sizes, shapes, colors, and textures. They may appear as we walk down the street, through a shopping mall, or across a parking lot. I have been called by stones from a young age. I did not know why, but they just spoke to me.

Stones volunteer to be of assistance. Each stone has its own qualities. The stones that call to us will let us know their way of service. Some stones excel at healing, some for grounding, some for extraction or for divination. They will let us know for whom and how they can be of service. We must just listen.

Stones may allow for discernment and divination of the cause of illness, of turmoil, or of the journey of the soul. We blow the essence of who we are into a stone and then ask the spirit of this stone for guidance. First, we explore the stone as it is. We observe its physical characteristics through our senses. What is the texture of the stone? Is it smooth, or rough? Are there colors? Are they bright or dull? Is there a taste of sweetness or bitterness as we touch the stone to our tongue? Does the stone carry a fragrance? Is it invigorating? Is it stagnant? Do we breathe deep of its essence, or hold our breath? Is there a voice heard from the stone that tells us of our path?

Next, we shift our awareness to the mind. We become aware of our emotions and our state of being. We begin to interpret the energy of the stone. Perhaps we may become aware of a sense of adventure, of aliveness, or of sadness and fear.

We then move from the mind and interpretation into the metaphors of life. Here the stone may reveal to us an awareness of the mythic journey we are experiencing. Or perhaps, we may have access to our myths of creation and the journey of our soul.

Stones offer themselves as healers. There are stones which contain energy that brings strength and nourishment to our energetic field. There are stones that serve as portals or gateways so that we may journey to other realms and dimension. A stone may be used to perform a *limpia*—a process in which heavy or foreign energies are extracted from the body. This process is a cleansing of the physical body, the emotional body, and the energetic body. The stone placed on the surface of the body, or brought into the energetic field, acts as a magnet, drawing out energy that has created a disruption to the flow of our life force. This blockage perhaps appears in the form of a belief, contract, or judgment that no longer serves us.

Stones are born of the earth. They receive the heavy energy we offer. They, just like Mother Earth, will digest this energy we have given to them and, in return, offer back to us energy that we may use as sustenance for our journey. This is an act of ayni.

CHAPTER EIGHT

THE MEDICINE WHEEL

The path I am walking is the path of the medicine wheel. The medicine wheel is a journey. It is a journey to walk in consciousness and with awareness. It is a journey to remember who we are. It is a journey to reclaim our power, our innocence, and to re-remember the wisdom of our ancestors, past, present, and future. It is a journey to walk into the forgotten realms of our being. It is a journey of creation, a journey of growth, and a journey of evolution. It is the journey of our soul.

The medicine wheel symbolizes the journey of healing. It is a map through which we may orient ourselves to our journey of wholeness and health. While each culture may attach different beliefs, teachings, or names to each step on this journey, the archetypal journey to wholeness and health is the same.

The medicine wheel is a multidimensional, multidirectional structure that may shift up and down along a central axis. The medicine wheel is constantly evolving, constantly changing. It is representative of who we are at any given moment. The medicine wheel is a map that contains the tools for the journey our soul is walking.

The medicine wheel is anchored by the four cardinal directions of the compass, by Mother Earth below and Father Sky above. Influenced and balanced by the power of these archetypal energies, healing may manifest. Each anchor is associated with an archetype and the energy of that archetype. As we call upon these archetypal powers, a sacred vessel is created. This sacred vessel is often referred to as sacred space. Our soul and physical being when in balance with self, community, and spirit occupy the center of this sacred vessel in a state of balance that manifests health and well-being.

The goal of our journey through the medicine wheel is that we grow, we evolve, and that we may stand in the middle of this wheel. Here, in the center of the medicine wheel, we are informed by the insights and energies of all the directions and by the consciousness of Mother Earth and of the heavens. Here we are not only in balance with the axis of creation, but we become the axis of creation.

The journey around the medicine wheel is ongoing. Each rotation brings us knowledge, learning, and healing at a higher level. As we go around the wheel, we are no longer caught for long periods by issues or behaviors but recognize and solve the problem in front of us faster and from a different level so that we may return to that place of balance in the center of the medicine wheel.

Each of the four directions of the medicine wheel represents insights and practices which must be embodied by a person on their path to healing. Each insight, each practice represents a quantum of energy that, when integrated within our luminous energy field, allows us to experience life fully, to live in right relationship with our self, our community, and the source of creation.

Each of the directions and archetypes carry with it an archetypal energy. Archetypal energy as defined by Jung may be described as a collectively inherited, unconscious idea, a pattern of thought or image, a knowing that is universally present in the essence of an individual. The wise healer, the beautiful maiden, knowing fear. Each is different for every one of us, yet we all know what they are.

Archetypes are powerful forces found within and outside the universe. They are primordial energies of creation that exist outside of time and space and yet manifest within time and space to bring order, healing, and harmony to all that is. These are the organizing powers and forces that have created the galaxies and the universe.

Though the appearances and names of the archetypes may differ from culture to culture, even perhaps amongst individuals, the universal energy they represent and bring forth are the same. The shaman calls upon these forces to assist in bringing balance to the energies of his client and of the universe. We, too, may connect to these primordial energies to receive and be informed by their guidance, medicine, and wisdom.

The archetypal energies of the medicine wheel in the tradition in which I was trained are represented in the four directions of the compass by serpent, jaguar, hummingbird, and condor, in the world below by Mother Earth, and in the world above by Father Sky and Inti Taita, the Sun. The shaman develops a working relationship with these energies to bring forth healing and balance. We, too, may work in ceremony with the archetypes of the medicine wheel to transform the energies of fear, hate, anger, and of all the emotions that lower the vibration of our being, into energy of the finest vibration.

Find a quiet spot where you will not be disturbed. Invite the archetypal energies of the medicine wheel to sit with you, to be with you. Embody their nature. Sense what it is like to be a serpent as you connect belly to belly to Mother Earth. Or to fly like an eagle soaring on the wind. Let their nature, their medicine inform the essence of your soul.

When we call upon serpent, jaguar, or one of the other archetypal energies, they will appear in our life to bring balance to our state of being. When we are in balance with self, community, and spirit, we call this state of being health.

CHAPTER NINE

DIRECTIONS OF THE MEDICINE WHEEL

I present the teachings of the medicine wheel as it was taught to me and as I have interpreted the journey. This is a journey, and a story of enlightenment and awareness of the stories we tell and of the death that we are living. This is a journey about shedding this death and the stories that limit our life. This is a journey of life and of rebirth. This is a journey on which we reconnect with the essence of self, and a story of triumph. This is a story of a journey without a beginning and without an end, a journey of death and renewal.

The journey around the wheel allows one to incorporate the archetypical energy, the practices, and the teachings of each direction. We can move back and forth and above and below. We can look from above to see our destination and where we might need to work. From the lower world, we have awareness of the subconscious beliefs and judgments that shape our reality. In the South, we become aware of the stories we have created that define and restrict our own growth.

In the West, we see which of these beliefs or myths we call reality need to die. In the North, we see the gifts of our ancestors and of our lineages. Gifts that will bring sustenance for the journey of our soul. In the East, we experience the birth of our new beginnings and our new journey.

Through the illusions of time, we witness the cycles of the universe and the seasons of life. Each morning with the birth and rising of a new yet constant sun, we witness an act of creation. Each evening we witness death and a shedding of what was or might have been as the sun sets into the great void. Within these same cycles we may experience times of rest as we lie fallow, nourishing, preparing ourselves for what might be. Or perhaps we may experience times of great turbulence or of great joy as the processes of birth and renewal bring forth new life and possibilities.

The South, Awareness of What Is

The South is a time of awareness. A time in which we become aware of our wounded self. A time in which we become aware of the stories that we have created to justify this wounded self.

The South is a time for healing and shedding these stories that no longer serve our journey. These are the stories that have stalled or derailed our journey through life. These are the stories that have kept the wounds of our past festering like an open sore.

The journey of the South may begin at a time of crisis. A time when awareness heralds the need for us to change the stories we have told and become, if there is to be life. The journey of the South is supported by the practices of non-suffering, of non-attachment, and through finding the perfection and beauty of the moment we are experiencing in life.

Non-suffering means we give up the story and suffering attached to an event. We no longer write the story of our victimhood, of our grief, or of our sad lot in life. We become the author of a new story. We write the story of the hero, where we have learned our lessons and we have healed our wounds.

Non-attachment means we let go not only of the roles we have created in the story but also of the validation and identity they give us in life. We release the stories and dictates that society has given to us. We become the storyteller, the myth-maker of a new reality.

With awareness comes choice. We choose to source from beauty. We find the beauty, the gift, and the teaching of the moment. We choose to experience beauty where others may see misfortune, pain, and victimhood. We welcome the opportunity for growth and healing that we have been presented by that which is occurring in our life.

The archetypal energy of the South is serpent. This is the energy of wisdom, sexuality, and healing. It is the binding principle of union and creation. It is fertility. Serpent is the literal lens of reality. It is where "everything is as it appears to be." There is no alternate meaning.

When we call upon the archetypal energies of serpent, we have access to the wisdom and knowledge of our inner self. The nature of the serpent allows her to delve deeply into the nooks and crannies of our unconsciousness. Through her exploration she may unearth the hidden shadows and restrictive beliefs created by past events and traumas that are woven within the fabric of our inner being. The beliefs and shadows that unconsciously guide us through life.

As humans, we have created a thick and calloused skin, composed of old traumas and beliefs that keep us tied to the past in a stagnation of energy that no longer supports life. The instinctual drive of serpent to survive directs her to shed this old skin when it becomes too restrictive for her to continue to live or to move forward. When we call upon the spirit of serpent, we, too, may shed the skins of our past that we may live a life renewed. A life that is unencumbered by the stories and suffering we have created around the events and traumas of our life. Through this shedding serpent brings fertility to our dreams and undertakings. Through the instinctual nature of serpent, we may once again experience the bounty of life.

Let us take a moment, review our present life, and see how serpent might bring balance to our life. What are the stories, the beliefs, and the judgments that have become too restrictive for us to live with? Where are we in need of new energy on this journey of life? Let us call upon the instinctual energies of serpent to help us shed the skin, the stories, the beliefs, and the judgments that have stagnated our life. Once shed, a new life force will begin to flow and bring fertility to our journey of transformation.

The West, Death of What Has Been

The West is the way of the luminous warrior. It is the light of this warrior that illuminates the shadows and unconscious beliefs of our life. The luminous warrior has no enemies in this life. The luminous warrior sees these supposed enemies for who they are. They are just energy that has been assigned the quality of fear, of anger, or of the unknown. We may call upon the luminous warrior within to guide us as we journey into the unknown realms of life.

The journey of the luminous warrior is supported by the practices of fearlessness, certainty, non-doing, and non-engagement. Fear and darkness are infused with light. The world is engaged with love and light. This is the pure love of munay, of agape, not romantic love. The world is engaged with the highest frequencies of energy. Adversity becomes harmonized and is seen, is honored as the teacher of our soul.

Certainty means we close the back doors. We no longer waste energy by wondering about the "what ifs." What if we had married this person or that one? What if we choose this action or another? We know with certainty that the universe will provide and support us in whatever path we choose with opportunity for growth and evolution of our soul. It will be up to us, however, to be open to the learning and opportunity.

Non-doing means we flow with the current of the Universe. We no longer micromanage our lives. We no longer force change. We no longer try to change what will change itself. Change happens when and as it is meant to occur.

Non-engagement means we choose not to engage in the battles. Instead, we strive to connect with our enemies and achieve a common goal. Our differences become fertile ground for harmony and understanding of opposites as we come together in unity.

The archetypal energy of the West manifests through the instinctual nature of the jaguar. In the jungles of the Amazon, jaguar represents the catalyst between life, death, and renewal as she instinctively preys upon the weak and the old. Jaguar intimately knows the rainbow bridge that connects between the realms of life and death. She knows this path without need for an anchor or guide. She can leave this world and physical body and return without warning. It is this power of sudden death and the resultant change that brings forth the rapid renewal of our life force. This interplay creates a dynamic balance between life and death that allows for the young and the healthy to thrive while the weak and the old perish.

Jaguar is the emotional lens of reality and where "nothing is as it appears to be." Jaguar allows crisis to become opportunity, death to become a gateway to life. The medicine of jaguar, when called upon, brings forth sudden transformation and change. Jaguar devours the heavy energies of our life such as anger, fear, guilt, or shame, but may also call upon us to experience these same emotions that we may become aware and heal an underlying wound. She will pounce without warning upon her prey. We must be ready to adapt or perish when she visits.

We may call upon the medicine of jaguar to keep us alive and renewed both as individuals and as a species. When we call upon jaguar, we connect with the power of renewal and the forces of life and death that allow for life to persist in a changing yet unchanging environment. These are the forces and power of sudden change, sudden death, and the resultant transformations that will bring forth transcendence and new life.

As we call jaguar into our life, we may ask, "What are the beliefs, the patterns, or the myths that must be preyed upon and let to die so we may move forward on our journey of life and empowerment?"

The North, the Birth of What Is to Be

The North is the way of the seer, the visionary, and the creator. The North is a journey of growth and of evolution for our self and for our soul. The North offers us the opportunity to create a new self—free of ego, free of the myths and beliefs of others.

In the North, we become the weavers of our own myths of creation. Myths that speak to our soul and guide our journey through life. In the North as we create and embody these new myths, we may bring forth a new set of maps and an internal compass that is trued for our journey. A compass and set of maps that will guide us as individuals and as a collective into a reality of our own creation. A reality where we are bathed in joy, beauty, and compassion, where we live in ayni and are nourished by the sweet nectars of life.

When we choose to open our vision and ourselves to the North direction of the medicine wheel, we find that we have access to the wisdom and teachings of ancient beings and to the voices and dreams of our children's children. The understanding of these teachings and the embodiment of this wisdom are facilitated by the practices of beginner's mind, transparency, integrity, and the practice of living life consequentiality.

The practice of beginner's mind means we let go of our beliefs and expectations. We experience life and its events as if for the first time. We have no preconceived notions of the outcome we are about to experience in this moment or the next.

The practice of transparency allows us to be seen. When we live in transparency, our talk and our actions equal who our soul knows us to be. When we are transparent we are authentic; in authenticity we allow vulnerability. For when we no longer hide who we are from ourselves or from others, then we are seen for who we are. When we practice transparency we are, perhaps for the first time, disrobed of the myths and beliefs of others that we may know our authentic self.

To live in integrity we must go beyond just speaking our truth; we must live our truth. When we live life in integrity, we admit our mistakes, we take responsibility for our mistakes, and we act to correct the mistakes we have made. When we live life in integrity, we come into right relationship with ourselves, our communities, and Spirit. We are in ayni with life and with the cosmos.

To live consequentially, we live life in awareness. We know through awareness we have a choice; we have a choice as to how we react or respond to situations in life. We recognize the impact that our actions, thoughts, and intentions have on the universe. We know our thoughts are energy, direct energy, that may manifest an unintended outcome. When we choose to live consequentially, we choose to manifest peace, joy, beauty, and love to guide our life.

The archetypal energy of the North is hummingbird. As we call upon the archetypal energy of the hummingbird, we may connect with the wisdom and myths of our ancestors and the voices of our children. These are the myths and voices that feed and nourish our soul. The myths that carry us through the journeys of our life with ease and with courage as the songs of joy, peace, and laughter bring forth the flowers of life that nourish us along the way. These are the flowers and sweet nectar of life that provide us the courage to complete this journey and the strength to no longer return to that which no longer feeds the soul.

The instinctual characteristics of the hummingbird allow her to observe while in flight or in the stillness of motion. She flies forward, backward, side to side, stops in midflight, all while looking forward, observing, seeing what is, and the effect of what has been. The hummingbird reveals to us the journey of our soul. When we call upon the energy of hummingbird to be with us, we open ourselves to awareness and see our soul's journey through the lens of our heart. A journey of our soul that many might see as impossible, yet that our soul has been called upon to undertake by Spirit.

A journey that brings forth growth and evolution of our self and of our being. A journey that reconnects us with the ancestors of our past and the children of our future who have yet to manifest physically in this realm of being we call life. This is a journey of wholeness and of health. It's a journey of love and of light, a journey to bring us back to our heart, to that place of unconditional love that the Q'ero call munay.

The universe will always provide for us what we need, when we need it, and manifest it just as we need it to be at any given moment of life. Through the lens of hummingbird, "Everything is as it is at the moment." A stone may be a tool for writing, a weapon, or a means to create music. We may call upon the medicine of the hummingbird to renew our life force, to reconnect us with our own instinctual drives, and to lead us to the sweet nectar of life that will feed our soul. Through the magic and vision of hummingbird, we may experience joy, beauty, and the courage to see the opportunity provided to us in each moment and with each breath that we take.

Let us take a moment to assess honestly the state of our life force, as we ask, "What are the flowers or the myths of life that no longer feed our soul? Where do we need renewal of our life force? Where is our soul parched for life? Who or what consumes our life energy? Who or what no longer brings joy or beauty into our life?"

Then let us call upon the instinctual energies of the hummingbird to help us find the flowers that now feed us. The flowers whose nectar bring nourishment and sustenance to our soul and provide us the courage to move forth on our journey.

The East, the Birth of What Is New

The East is the way of the sage. The sage is one who not only holds the wisdom of the ages but shares this wisdom with all who seek it. In the East, we give ourselves to Spirit; we become one with Spirit. In the East, our mind becomes silent as our soul perceives the miracle of life.

In the East, we are Spirit creating. When we dream a world of joy, we lay the foundation of a matrix on which joy may manifest.

When we dream a world of integrity, we create the milieu for integrity to exist. In the East, when we dream, our dream becomes the reality we create.

The way of the sage is supported by the practice of mastery of time, of owning one's projections, of no mind, and of indigenous alchemy. When we step out of linear time, we step into circular or sacred time. Here time moves like a wheel, and the future can influence the past just as the past can affect the future. We find the cause of a present event may well be in the future. The shaman works in this realm of sacred time to heal and to shift destiny.

When we own our projections about life, we become aware that our beliefs, conscious and unconscious, create our world. Taking ownership and acknowledging our projections allow us to release our limiting beliefs and create a world of possibility. A world in which we are no longer victim, a world in which we may thrive and create wholeness and health.

In the process of no mind, we must break free of our thoughts and ask, "Who is asking this? Who is thinking this?" When we no longer identify with our mind, only the sage, only Spirit remains. Remember, our mind creates stories often out of fear and scarcity.

In the East, we begin to understand the practice of indigenous alchemy, which is comprised of four steps. These steps allow us to identify, differentiate, integrate, and transcend the energy of the issues we face. The process of indigenous alchemy is the journey of the medicine wheel. We identify the story we have created. We realize we are not our story. We bring forth new empowering stories and myths that we begin to weave into our being. We transcend our old self as the new self is created.

The archetypal energy of the East is a marriage between the eagle and the condor. Eagle and condor are the wings upon which we may soar to new heights, new elevations, and new realities. They allow us to see beyond the mountains and obstacles in front of us so that we may envision the future. The energy of the East is an energy of clarity, vision, foresight, transformation, and transcendence. When we are in balance and right relationship, this energy allows us to soar from the hold of past trauma, to see, to create, and to soar into a destiny of joy and beauty, of wholeness and health, and of love and light.

Indigenous legend prophesizes that the eagle and condor will fly together as one to heal Mother Earth. Healers of the Andes and of North America say the eagle and condor are emissaries to and of Spirit, that they are the forces of transcendence who represent the power to evolve beyond oneself for the benefit of self and of all. This is the realm through which the will of Spirit manifests. This symbolic flight is a coming together of the Western and indigenous ways to create health and wholeness for all of creation.

I witnessed this transformation over the ancient temple at Yaynu, east of the Cordillera Blanca in northern Peru, as the energy of the condor and the blue Ancash eagle transcended duality to fly in unity as one. Here, as we called upon the spirits of the land, working with the spirit of wachuma and the archetypal energies of eagle and condor, unity manifested. They were one.

Now ask yourself, "How is my vision blocked?" or "Where can I not see past the mountains of my life?" Then call upon the instinctual energies of the eagle and of the condor to allow the soul to soar high above these obstacles to see the possibilities. Call upon their instinctual nature as birds of prey to hunt with keen vision to find their prey, then to swoop in from high above and remove any obstacles with their claws and talons.

Pachamama

Mother Earth, Pachamama, is the force and power of the feminine. She is the womb, the receptive vessel from where all life may manifest. She is the field in which the seeds of our dreams may be planted, nourished, and grown into reality.

Mother Earth is always present. She is the force which receives and mulches the heavy energies of our life, the emotions, the trauma, and the turmoil we experience. As we walk this path of healing and of life, she is the foundation, our constant in life. She will never leave.

Now might be a good time to ask of ourselves, "Where do we feel abandoned in life? What are the emotions, the traumas, or the stories of life that we continue to hold onto, that no longer serve us? Are these the stories of betrayal, of defectiveness, or of unworthiness?" When we choose to release these stories and be-liefs to Mother Earth, we call upon her instinctual nature to mulch and transform these energies into fertilizer and nutrients that will feed, nourish, and germinate the seeds of our dreams.

Father Sky

Father Sky, Inti Tai Ta, the Sun is the creative power of the uni-verse. Father Sky is the power of the masculine, the creator of the universe. Father Sky is active and in motion, constantly changing. Within Father Sky are the stars, the planets, and the sun, which represent the cycles of the universe, the cycles of life, the cycles of the year, and the cycles of the day. Father Sky is the bringer of the new day, the crops, and new life.

Ask of the self, "What in my life is nearing the end of a cycle, or is ready to begin a new cycle?" Then we may call upon the en-ergies of Father Sky to prepare and guide us through these cycles of change.

Now that we have connected to the gifts and the power of each archetype, we may continue to work with these archetypes to create new visions and new realities—realities that will feed and nourish our souls. We may use their medicine, their powers of transformation, to transform and transcend the reality of the myths and beliefs we or others have created. We may step into what is possible, not what is probable.

CHAPTER TEN

A SHAMANIC JOURNEY

A shamanic journey allows us to experience the realms of our shadow and of the unknown. These are the realms of consciousness that most may never experience. These are the realms of the imaginal. The realms of our original self, untouched by illness, disease, or turmoil. The realms where we may connect with the spirits of our guardians, the spirit of an illness, or where we may reconnect to a self that is healed.

The ability to journey without the mind is the difference between a trip and a journey. A trip might be described as traveling from one place to another. The purpose of a trip may be business, pleasure, or perhaps leisure. We might take a trip across the country, across town, or even to another continent. Our mind influences the events of a trip. We plan a trip. We have an itinerary. We have a preconceived idea of where we are going, what we might experience. There is a timetable for each moment, each day.

The ability to journey without the filters and influence of the mind is an important process in the understanding and integration of our journey through life. We have all experienced the energy of a trip; far fewer have experienced the energy of a journey.

A journey is something more than a trip across the country. A journey is something we embark upon, we prepare for; it is a pilgrimage for our soul. Within the shamanic parlance, journeying takes us from the known realms of our mind and into the realms of the unknown. The word *journey* itself is imbued with mystery, and perhaps the promise of a life-changing experience as we journey to unknown places and into far-off lands that we call enchanted.

Shamanic journeying may be self-guided or facilitated by a shaman. In the latter case, the shaman either guides an individual on their journey or embarks and walks this journey on behalf of an individual. When walked for another, the shaman brings the energy of the journey back to the individual, perhaps blowing this energy into the chakras, weaving it into their field of energy, or in helping the client to write a new myth of creation.

Journeying allows us an opportunity to speak with the spirit of an illness so we may understand the presence of this illness in our life. Journeying allows us to speak to our soul. We may be shown our soul's journey. We may find that an illness is part of the soul's agreement to evolve and to grow. We may discover the archetypal wounds or themes we have chosen to experience and perhaps heal in this lifetime. We may remember that long before entering this lifetime, we had chosen that a terminal illness would be our vehicle of choice to transcend this physical body and enter other realms of being.

We journey with intent. The intent may be to discover the source of our wounds, to recover lost soul parts, to speak with the spirit of an illness, or to meet with our healed self. Journeying creates a stage on which one can meet the healed self, merge with the healed self, and be the healed self. The journey allows us to access a mythical realm that occurs outside of time and space. The journey itself may be surreal, as if a dream. Yet it is seen.

It is the act of seeing that creates. When we see ourselves in illness, we create illness. When we see ourselves in health, we create health. By seeing, even if only in our mind's eye, we are creating and energizing a possibility in which we may create health. I have had clients scheduled for surgery who, in a dream, have seen themselves in the healed state, and then, when they present for surgery, the pathology is no longer present.

For these individuals, the healed state had been discovered outside of ordinary time, in a journey of their dreams. Energized by the fact that it was seen, the healed state then manifested within the physical reality of their body. The act of their seeing health and wholeness during their dream allows for the possibility of health to become a reality. We see health. We witness a state of health. We then manifest health.

In the Andean cosmology, there is no distinction between the symbolic and the actual. They are one and the same. Whether a result of a guided journey, or of a dream, when there is symbolic change, the actual changes. Illnesses are deeply held beliefs that may manifest as disharmony in our life. During a journey, we may be shown the beliefs that prevent us from healing or that have created the disease within us. These beliefs may appear in metaphor, in image, or as a symbol of the literal event in one's life. We work with and within the metaphors and symbols to bring balance and healing to our soul and to our being that we may create health.

Chapter Eleven

The Untethered Journey

During my first experiences with the void, I created blockages and anchors. Creations of my own fear—fear that my ego, that I, would be consumed by the void. Blockages that stopped me from entering the vortex. Anchors that kept me tethered to this reality. Later, I was told by wachuma, "When I choose to return or stay for myself, not for someone else, then I will die to who I am." I had promised my daughter Alicia that I would return. I would not die. To experience the void, we must die fully to who we are. I was never truly free to experience the death of who I was. I understand now that these anchors were of my own need, my own creation.

In April 2016, we visited Chavín de Huántar, an ancient temple in northern Peru dedicated to the medicine and teachings of the sacred plant wachuma. Informed and held by the spirits of the temple, we offered our prayers and ourselves to the ancestors of this ancient site. A site some believe was seeded from the stars, impregnated by the extraterrestrial spirit of the Lanzón, to become the birthplace of humanity and the culture of the Chavín.

Here in Chavín, I returned to beyond the void of creation, yet this time devoid of anchors, tethers, and connection to Alicia. The spirit of the medicine had said, "When I choose to return or when I choose to stay for myself, not for someone else, then I will fully die to who I am." This night I crossed without a tether or an anchor into the void and returned because I chose to return. I had died to who I was.

I found my path across the rainbow bridge and back again. This was the death of my soul. Many years later, deep in the jungles of Peru, I experienced the final death, the death of spirit. If we are to return from this final death, the death of the spirit, we must be fully conscious as we make this journey. I returned, awakened to a new vision, a new journey of life.

This untethered journey into the void and back is the legend and lore of Choque Chinchay and the rainbow bridge. This is the jaguar that moves freely between the worlds and the realms of life and death. These are the realms of the manifest and the unmanifest. When we have completed this journey, alone and untethered, we, too, have access to the rainbow bridge, the bridge that exists between the realms of life and death.

My work with wachuma has allowed me to remember that we source from the void of creation, the void from which the unmanifest energy of creation flows forth. It is the void from which essence and form manifest out of nothingness into somethingness, or from somethingness into nothingness.

When we source from the void, we may create our own reality. We are the creator and the creation. We may create a universe with clear vision and intent. We remember that we are the gods and goddesses; that we are children of the light and the children of the stars. We remember that we are no different from the stones, the rivers, or the canyons; that we are no different from the planets, the distant stars, or the ancient galaxies.

From the unmanifest energy of creation, we may create a universe where all is possible. We may create a universe where joy and beauty abound, where both compassion and courage exist. A universe fed with abundance and balance. A universe of wholeness and health, a universe sourced from love and light. A universe that is in ayni, in right relation with all that is. It is into this void that the shaman journeys on behalf of his clients and the cosmos to release the form of what has been and bring forth healing and harmony for all.

CHAPTER TWELVE

CORE HEALING TECHNIQUES

Illumination, extraction, and soul retrieval are the core healing practices taught in the Healing the Light Body School to bring one back into health and right relationship. The essence and intent of these modalities source directly from the ancient healers who inhabited the Andes and the indigenous communities of the Americas. It has been my honor to learn and experience these healing practices directly from the descendants of these medicine men and women—healers who have chosen to share their wisdom, knowledge, and ways with open hearts.

Illumination

The illumination process combusts the heavy energies found within the energetic organs of our body called chakras. These heavy energies are often a result of an unresolved wounding or trauma we have experienced that may have scarred the energetic matrix of our body.

Each chakra directly informs and is responsible for the function of that part of the endocrine and central nervous system it is associated with. Dysfunction of a chakra, whether a result of blockage or imbalance, may bring forth illness, disease, or turmoil in our life. In the Andes this process of cleansing the heavy energies from the chakras is called *hucha mikhuy*.

Once this heavy energy is consumed and transformed, the pure light of Spirit found within the eighth chakra is brought into the affected chakra. (The eighth chakra is found outside our physical body, yet within our energetic field, and is directly sourced from Spirit.) As we direct this light of Spirit from our eighth chakra and into the affected chakra, the underlying scar is healed and erased from the energetic matrix.

Illumination is an energetic process that shifts the matrix of the energetic field. The illumination process releases the heavy energy and blockages, allowing the chakra to come back into balance. As the energetic field and chakra(s) are illuminated with the light of Spirit, healing and balance occur. This renewed state of balance creates harmony that is essential for wholeness and health.

Extraction

Intrusive energy may be wispy and fluid or fixed and solid. When solid, this energy is described as crystallized. Crystallized energy usually results when we are under a continual barrage of energy from a source that our bodies perceive as hostile. This energy is often unintentionally projected as anger, envy, or jealousy toward us from one who means us no harm. We, too, may in fact be the source of this energy as we unconsciously or consciously blame ourselves for actions we have taken. Under this constant barrage of energy, the defense systems of the LEF are overwhelmed, and these energies may enter our luminous or physical body to become crystalized, resulting in the blockage of the vital force.

Crystallized energy may take the form of a symbolic object. When someone is betrayed, we might find a dagger stuck in the back, or a noose around the neck of one being choked in a relationship. Crystallized energy is like petrified wood and cannot be consumed or removed through the illumination process alone. It must be removed manually. Though this process is separate, removal of this crystallized energy is done in conjunction with an illumination in order to loosen, cleanse, and consume the energy holding the crystallized energy in place and to release the affinity for this energy in the future.

Intrusive energy that is wispy and fluid may move through our physical and energetic body. This energy, which may be a thought form or an emotion, may take on a personality and consciousness of its own, consuming its host in fear, anger, depression, or even illnesses that may not respond to the intervention offered by Western traditions. In contrast, intrusive entities are souls that have been disincarnated from a human body yet have not transitioned back to the realms of their ancestors. This may occur when a person dies traumatically or under the influence of anesthesia or narcotics.

It is not uncommon for these disincarnate souls to be a deceased relative or friend who has come to us for help, perhaps even unaware that they have died. While not intending to do harm, just as the mistletoe enters into a parasitic relationship with the oak tree, the intrusive entity attaches itself to one of the host's chakras. Then it establishes a direct connection to the endocrine and central nervous system of the host, who may begin to experience vague and unusual psychological and physical symptoms. The host may even develop the personality or physical ailments of a deceased being.

Intrusive energies and entities are removed using an extraction crystal or at other times the death rites. This is followed by an illumination to change the affinity of the client; otherwise, the individual will just continue to attract similar energies. When we change the affinity, it is equivalent to installing a new lock. The entity will not have access unless we offer them the new key. The final step in the extraction process is the guiding of the disincarnate souls back to the spirit world, where the luminous healers will assist these souls in healing and in a return to consciousness. Intrusive energy is returned to Mother Earth, where it is assimilated and mulched back into nutriments that will feed her.

Soul Loss

Throughout our lifetimes, we may have encountered soul loss. Soul loss may cause us to live a life in which we continually repeat unhealthy patterns or choices. Soul loss occurs when, as the result of physical or emotional trauma, a portion of our soul disassociates or splinters off so that it may survive. The disassociation of a child who is abused or a soldier suffering post-traumatic stress syndrome from battle may be such examples of soul loss. Once this soul piece has disassociated, it is not available to us and we are not in balance. We are in disharmony and susceptible to illness or turmoil.

When we treat an illness that is a result of soul loss with medications only, the illness and accompanying symptoms may be alleviated. However, until there is healing of our soul, our inner spirit, we are susceptible to the manifestation of further disease and turmoil.

Soul loss may also occur when at times of unhappiness or emotional fatigue we leave parts of our soul at a place or time whose memory brings us solace or joy. In these scenarios we may be fed by the memories of the past, but we are unable to generate joy from the events of the present.

We may also be responsible for soul loss in another, as we are unable or unwilling to release the soul of a loved one who is attempting to cross over at death; believing our reluctance to release our loved one is from love. To be sure, soul loss occurs not just at times of trauma but may occur in times of joy as we give parts of our self to another, perhaps to our partner in love.

Soul loss is not limited to individuals. Characteristics attributed to soul loss may cross generational lines or be found in families, cities, and cultures. It is even held in our Western mythology that as a society we experienced and carry forward the wounding and loss of our innocence that resulted as we were cast from the primordial Garden of Eden.

Soul Retrieval

The indigenous peoples of the Andes believe there are three worlds of reality. These are not physical places but archetypical and energetic domains. The upper world is our future, the place of our destiny. It is where Spirit resides. The middle world is the present, where we and our families reside. It consists of the visible and invisible worlds. The lower world is our past, where all human history resides; it is the realm of lost souls and the womb of the great mother.

The lower world is where that loving, trusting, innocent part of us fled during a time of great conflict or trauma, leaving the wounded self behind. Here in the womb of the great mother, the soul part has sought and found refuge, waiting until it may once again be safe to return. This fragment of our soul is a packet of energy that is no longer available to us.

The space created when this piece of the soul fragmented may be filled with a limiting belief. A belief that whispers, "I am not worthy, I am defective..." Or perhaps it is an emotion that governs our life, such as fear, doubt, anger, guilt, etc., creating a world and a reality that are now unsafe.

It is not necessarily the literal event that occurred at the time of wounding that is the issue. It is how our body perceives and holds onto the event. As a result of its occurrence, a contract is formed. An example of a contract may be an individual who is unable to trust due to an early childhood trauma of perceived betrayal. This contract becomes the new operating system, creating a reality in which an individual may be unable to trust that they are worthy of love or that they are able to commit themselves to a relationship. This contract that initially may have been protective and healthy, after time, and in different circumstances, may become limiting and restrictive. Most frequently, these soul fragments will retreat to our subconscious and into the womb of the mother. We may journey to the lower world to observe the original wounding, the original event that caused this part of the soul to seek safety elsewhere, and to recover these fragments of our soul.

We journey with intent into our subconscious, the lower world, into the womb of our mother. We journey to become whole. We journey to observe the original wounding, to observe and change our limiting contracts. We journey to retrieve the fragments of our soul, the packets of energy that have been unavailable to us. Along the way, we may acquire gifts or a guide, perhaps a power animal to assist us in reintegrating these soul fragments and in doing so bring forth a new empowering contract to guide us through life. Soul retrieval must be embraced at the mythic, at the level of the soul. Otherwise, it is only an intervention that is a temporary fix for the mind.

To embody and embrace the healing of this journey into our subconscious, we must feel safe, and we must be safe. We must have healed the unresolved trauma that has continued to inform and to haunt our life. We must have shed the old beliefs and contracts that have shaped our myths of creation and our reality of the present. We must be ready to leave or have already left the toxic environment of our life. An individual who is abused will again suffer soul loss if they have not stepped from the environment of abuse. Prior to undertaking a journey to recover the soul, a shaman or therapist may need to assist an individual to make the necessary changes in their life. Perhaps to heal the beliefs and imprints surrounding worthiness.

Maps of the Lower World

There are different maps of the lower world. It is important to know the map and be familiar with the terrain we are working with. My access to the lower world is by a path that leads to a meadow in the invisible realm of this world, the world in which we live. Here there is an opening that descends through the layers of the earth until one arrives in a large underground meadow or garden. The map of the lower world with which I was trained and follow consists of a realm in which there is a garden. Within this garden is a gatekeeper who will grant one access to the unconscious and to the four chambers of the soul.

Once granted access to the four chambers of the soul, the shaman may find the source of the original wounding. The wound may be an event that happened in childhood, in the womb, or in the lifetime of an ancestor. There are players and actors in the chambers. The events and actors present are all aspects and manifestations of who we are. We can stop any player and they will tell us what is going on. What is revealed may be a metaphor for the original wounding or of how this trauma still informs the body. We may witness what happened but not fix it. It has occurred; we do not change the past, though we may perceive and reframe the events of the past through a new and empowering lens.

In the next chamber, we may find a soul contract. This is a contract made at a time of trauma and while under duress. The contract of how we promised we would live our life to avoid being hurt in the future. Not thought out, this contract is entered into at the moment of trauma. It is a promise we make for ourselves to assure survival. In this chamber, we have the opportunity to review and change this contract so we may begin to live a healthy life.

As we search further, we may find another chamber, a chamber in which the soul fragment that had splintered away may be found. Protected in this chamber, the fragment is waiting for the time that it will be safe to return home again. When reintegrated, the energy of this soul fragment allows us to once again be whole. In wholeness, we experience health. We experience joy, beauty, and a passion for life. To maintain this state, we must be willing to make the changes in our life that will support our growth.

We may find in the fourth chamber a gift. Perhaps it is representative of courage or certainty. The energies of this gift will help to nourish, reintegrate, and make it safe for the soul part to return and be embodied.

When returning from the four chambers, it is not unusual for a power animal to appear in this garden. The energies of this animal are archetypal. They will walk with us as we journey to health and wholeness.

This four-chambered map of the lower world has served me well. While in ceremony, purging may occur from above or below. One night, in the jungle outside of Iquitos, I found myself deeply involved with healing of the lower world. Metaphorically, I was releasing issues of my subconscious, the lower world, through my lower intestine. I repeatedly exited the ceremonial hut to evacuate the purge. Cautiously, I stepped down the wooden stairs, onto the sand in front of the hut, each time greeted in silence by one who was there to assist me, to guide me if necessary.

As I exited the *molaka*, a circular hut in which ceremony is held, there was a concrete bunker with four doors, four stalls, and four portals. Each door an entrance to a separate chamber of the soul. Deep in ceremony each stall became a viewing booth of my journey. Illuminated by the flickering light of a single candle, the images of my soul's journey would materialize from the sandy floor of the stall.

These were the images of events and lifetimes that spoke to me, that taught me and perhaps still held me hostage to what had been. I saw my wounding. I saw my contract. The lessons of my experiences exposed. I would now purge. I would literally purge the past from within to make room for the new.

The giraffe had come forth as my power animal. The legs of the giraffe are firmly grounded on the earth, offering the gift of a strong foundation. Her head reaching above the clouds and seeing into the heavens offers the gift of vision. This gift of vision allows for the future to be seen and the ability to gather the abundance of the teachings and of the harvest.

Metaphorically and literally I had been gifted a toilet during the journey, a throne from which to observe and rule my kingdom. My contract changed, fragments of the soul returned, and I was whole. Free of the limitations of the past, my destiny shifted. I could now become the benevolent king whom I had seen in my future.

Through the process of soul retrieval, the shaman intervenes at the level of the energetic and the mythic to create new maps for the journey of our soul. Maps that will allow us to experience joy and beauty. Maps that will provide an opportunity for us to rediscover the wholeness within our being. Maps that will allow us to reconnect with the pieces of ourselves which have always been there, yet unavailable. It is as in the song *Tin Man* by America implies, Oz did nothing. The wholeness of our being has always been with us. The shaman, just as the wizard, has only allowed us to reclaim our innate wholeness.

Chapter Thirteen

The Alchemy of Healing

The medicine wheel is a journey of alchemy. Alchemy, according to Webster, is "a power or a process that changes or transforms something in a mysterious and impressive way." At Yaynu as I witnessed the changing form of the eagle into the condor and back, I was witnessing the mystery of alchemy. This journey requires that we transform the energetic blockages created by our thoughts, beliefs, or judgments into nourishment for change.

In medieval times, it was believed by many that lead could be transformed to gold. Of course, this, so far, has not been proven true in Western reality. Yet the shamans and healers of yesterday and today know for a fact that alchemy is possible, and that alchemy is the basis of healing.

Mythology often casts the journey of healing as beginning in a garden where we have been entangled by the myths and beliefs of others. We are cast out of Eden. We are sentenced to live a life of toil and hardship. Our children, too, will suffer our karma. These myths create the stories and limiting beliefs that keep us trapped in a disempowering world.

The goal of indigenous alchemy is to transform into a source of power the old stories of victimhood and the myths of defectiveness and unworthiness.

The shamans know that the grief, sorrow, and victimhood a client presents with can be transformed from the heavy, disempowering emotions and stories into the rarified energies of joy and love. It is these rarified energies that allow an individual to live a life of empowerment and to create and grow the dreams of who they wish to be. The lead is transformed into gold.

This is indigenous alchemy. It is a power or process that allows us to identify, differentiate, integrate, and transcend the energy of the issues we face in a mysterious and impressive way. In other words, through the process of indigenous alchemy, the heaviness of life may be transformed into the beauty and radiance of gold.

Indigenous alchemy allows us to find beauty in all of creation. No longer are the imperfections of life seen as faults or defects; they are held as gifts and teachings along the path of our soul's growth and evolution. This is the gold.

CHAPTER FOURTEEN

STAGES IN THE JOURNEY

The process of healing and of alchemy is a journey. And as in all journeys, there are stages within the journey that occur and must be mastered before the journey can be completed. The first stage starts with the awareness of the need for a journey to begin. This is the calling. The calling is the whisper that gets louder and louder until we cannot deny its existence. We have identified there is an issue. Something must change, something must die, for us to live.

The second stage begins as we take the first step away from what has been. This is the departure. The departure is both the declaration of death and the proclamation of life. The death of what has been, and the birth of what can be. We differentiate. We step away from the issue. We remember that we have a choice as to how we experience life. This choice is the first step of the departure that must be undertaken by those on a journey of transformation.

The second step of the departure begins as we ask ourselves these questions: "If I could have my dreams, am I ready to transform the lead of my life into gold? What am I willing to change or give up in my life to obtain balance, health, joy, abundance, and beauty? Am I ready to forgive and hold those who I fault with compassion? Will I make the changes necessary in my life to support the growth of this new reality?"

On this journey of healing, we will be presented with many opportunities for growth and change. When we choose to bring back new myths and beliefs, we choose to heal. We choose to grow and evolve. We recognize pain happens in life, but we no longer create stories of suffering around this pain. We no longer create the myths and stories that disempower us or hold us hostage, a victim in the triangle of disempowerment (see below).

When we choose to heal, we no longer need to run away from life or life's circumstances. We take these opportunities to move forward and create new myths, new gods, and new beliefs that bring joy, beauty, compassion, love, and light into our life.

It is when we choose to keep the beliefs and the behaviors that have created disempowerment and suffering in our life that we do not heal. It is when we hold onto the myths and stories that limit us that we do not grow. It is when we continue to portray and hold ourselves as victim to our life's circumstances that we do not evolve.

Alchemy allows us to release what no longer serves us; to take responsibility for who and how we are. When we release the roles and beliefs that we and others have placed upon us, we no longer hold our ancestors, our parents, our karmic past, or our genetic inheritance accountable for our lot in life. We are no longer victim to life.

There may be obstacles we face along the way that make us rethink the need or desire for this journey. These obstacles herald the third stage of the journey. These obstacles are the tests that strengthen our resolve, and that once the journey has been completed will reward us with the radiance and luster of the gold. This is the stage of tests. As we master the tests and move forward on our journey, we begin to define and empower who we are becoming. Our new self is taking form. We begin to integrate what can be.

Once we have mastered the tests and have returned to where we began the journey, the journey is completed. This is the stage of return. The alchemical transformation has been performed. But it is not the one who left that has returned. When we return to the garden where we began the journey, we are not the same. We are no longer entangled in the myths of disempowerment or the beliefs of others. We now shine with the radiance and luster of gold. We have transformed our life from lead to gold. We have transcended the issue.

On this journey, there is always choice. To understand the full impact of our choices, we need to ask: "How do the beliefs that create our current reality serve who we are now? How does the status quo keep us safe? Is there a fear of failure? Is there a fear of change? Is there a fear of the death of our ego, the death of who we are or who we have been? Might there be fear of success or of who we could become?" These beliefs may need to be honored, heard, spoken, or just to be acknowledged before stepping forth.

We may choose to walk this journey with fear and doubt as our companions, or we may choose to walk in certainty. In certainty, there is no fear, there is no doubt, there is no anger, there is no guilt, there is only truth. When there is no anger, no doubt, then we have no enemies. We do not engage in battle with those along the way whose beliefs differ from ours. They are just different.

When we release doubt, there is no resistance to life's journey. We trust in the divine wisdom of the universe. We are free to ride the waves of the universe without trying to change them, without doing. We are free to create our own life, our own reality, no longer living a life dictated by the myths and fears of others. We no longer hold others accountable for the events or circumstances of our lives. Instead we take responsibility and ownership of our participation in these events.

CHAPTER FIFTEEN

THE STORIES WE ARE TELLING

Awareness and choice are two key essentials in the process of al-chemical transformation. Through awareness we become conscious of the stories we have created and that we tell to whomever will listen. Stories that we have told in many ways and on many stages throughout our lifetimes. These may be stories of disempowerment, of vulnerability, of betrayal, of separation, or of our defectiveness. These are the narratives from which we have created our life and to which we have unconsciously reacted and responded.

Awareness is a state of being in which we consciously bring forth into the light the stories and myths that have manipulated the unconscious basis for the beliefs we hold true. In awareness, we see how we are held by an event we have experienced or by a story we have created around an event. The need for awareness often reveals itself as an illness, or turmoil presents itself. The illness or turmoil then becomes an initiatory event in life—an event that brings forth an awakening to the fact that our life can no longer remain as it is. When we practice awareness, we become an observer of life rather than a victim of life. We take time to observe why we are who we are. We no longer react to the unknown; we discover our triggers.

Awareness offers us an opportunity to find the potential for growth and learning that life has presented us. Once we are aware, we have a choice. We may choose to become the victim of illness, of misfortune, of a terrible society or upbringing, or we may choose to depart on a journey of health and transformation.

When we choose the journey of health and transformation, we choose to empower ourselves. We choose to act. We begin to look at the beliefs and stories that have created illness or turmoil in our life. We see whose beliefs and whose reality we have been living. We own our part in the events of our life, but no longer allow them to own us. We become aware of the gifts these events have brought into our life. We take time to honor who we have been, and then to release the old forms so the new paradigms of our life may be born. We allow this work to integrate within the matrix of our being.

Take a moment now and in honesty and without judgment or attachment, ask yourself these questions: "What do I gain from being sick? What do I gain from being the victim? What do I gain from being angry? Am I ready to choose a different life, a life of love, of light, of abundance, of health, and of transformation?"

As we honor and release the stories we have held of victimhood, defectiveness, or unworthiness, we cease to identify with our illness or the events and beliefs of our life that have held us prisoner to what has been or is now. In this act of release, we free ourselves from the trajectory of these life stories. We transcend what was, the fate that has pushed us forward. We create an opportunity to transform how we see ourselves and how we are seen through the eyes of others. On this journey we open our-selves to the awareness of what we do want and no longer focus on what we lack. When we open to the mysteries of life and the universe, we may be surprised to discover that the gift of a termi-nal illness or the death of a relationship may be the freedom to experience life, itself, for the first time.

As this journey continues to unfold, there may be an oppor-tunity to drop the old stories and the myths which have influenced our beliefs and our reality. Our soul might once again remember the purpose of its journey through life. On this journey we may be given the opportunity to meet our healed self or call forth new myths of creation. These may be myths of empowerment that bring forth the essence of joy, beauty, wholeness, or health. In sha-manic lore, this is the hero's journey. A journey that leads us into and through the dark nights of our soul. It is a journey of aware-ness, courage, and endurance. It is the myth and journey of Parsifal and his quest for enlightenment and the Holy Grail.

Jung coined the phrase "wounded healer" to describe this jour-ney to health and wholeness. In this myth, we become aware of our wounding. We release how these wounds define us. We transcend these wounds to embody new realms and states of being.

When we have transcended our attachments to what is, or what was, we may look at our life without judgment. We may then respond from the depths of our soul as we ask, "What in my life no longer serves me? What do I desire instead? What is the per-sonal work I must do to manifest that which I desire? What are the changes I am prepared to make to maintain health and balance in my life?"

Listen to your soul—the soul holds the answers to these ques-tions and knows the work and changes needed to hold and anchor these new states of being. Changes that might include anything from establishing a practice of meditation to altering one's dietary intake.

As we step into this new realm of being, we may be tempted to share our gifts of wisdom and knowledge to empower others to begin their own journey of health and wellness. If we are so called, we share not as a rescuer but as a light of divine energy with grace, dignity, and respect.

It should be well noted that this process of awareness and choice is no more than a process and perhaps a waste of time and energy, unless we have first asked of ourselves these questions: "Whose dreams am I living now? Whose dreams will I be creating?" Only then—only when we have answered these questions honestly—may we begin to create a reality that is ours, and not the fulfilment of the dreams and desires cast upon us by another.

Chapter Sixteen

The Act of Seeing

The process of indigenous alchemy continues as we imagine what life might look like if we no longer accepted the consensual reality or the experiences of our family, our culture, or our society as truth. Imagery can be a powerful catalyst of healing. Just as poetry and song can speak to the heart of our soul to create myths of health and wholeness, images may also bring forth health and healing.

Just the act of seeing may energize, create, and manifest an outcome. When we journey, we step into that magical place outside of time and space, that place where all is seen, all is possible. We may see the origins of our myths and beliefs. We may see the origins of life. We may view our destiny. We may change our destiny before it occurs. We may connect with our healed self.

What might the vision of our life be if we allow ourselves to imagine a life in which we experience joy and beauty or a life in which forgiveness has occurred? What if we brought forth a lifetime in which we are nourished with love and light rather than one in which we are consumed by fear and hate? The possibilities and power of imagery to manifest our dreams know no bounds.

Let us find a quiet spot where we will not be disturbed, and then allow ourselves to enter a place of honesty and non-judgment from which we may observe and evaluate the myths and beliefs that have created our story of life.

We begin our journey as we ask that our breath carry us into a beautiful meadow, a meadow full of flowers, peace, and serenity. There is a river flowing through this meadow. We find a comfortable place to sit along the banks of this river or perhaps just to be held by the warmth of Mother Earth.

From this place of comfort and beauty, we call upon the archetypal energies of eagle. We connect with her gifts of vision and her ability to soar above the mundane events of this world in which we live. Free of judgment and attachment, we soar. We soar with her above the landscape of our life as we know it now, to be shown the expanse and panorama of our life as it is.

We see our life as it bubbles forth from Mother Earth, just as a spring sources to life from the walls of a canyon. We see our life as if a river, meandering through the countryside. We begin to observe as the essence and milestones of our life take form. We observe where we are now, who we are today, and where we may be taken tomorrow. We may see the origins of the beliefs and myths that have created our reality. We might ask and be shown whose myths, whose beliefs these are that have created the reality we are experiencing. We may recognize the myths and beliefs of our parents, our culture, or our society. We may see the beliefs we created at another time, how they served us then and how they no longer serve us now.

As we observe from above, we may honor these myths, these beliefs, and the reality in which we are held. Then we might ask, "Is this the reality that I have called forth, the reality that I desire?" We might release to the river that which no longer serves us, that it be carried away by the currents of this river.

We may ask to be shown and to connect with the essence of a new reality. A reality that will serve us now. Once we have connected with the essence of this new reality, we may see the current of the river bringing forth the new images, the new beliefs, the new truths we are willing to embrace that will support this new reality we will call life.

Let us bring these images of life, and the essence of change, back to our being, and follow our breath as it returns us once again back to this time, this place, and this body.

Life in Awareness

When we shift our beliefs and myths, when we release the stories of suffering and victimhood, and as we live with awareness and in stillness, we can access the possibilities of life. We remember that this act of seeing, even if only in our mind's eye, energizes, creates, and manifests an outcome. We release to the universe our vision. Then we allow the manifestation of this new reality to be manifested by the universe.

PART THREE

OF INTEGRATION AND UNDERSTANDING

THE JOURNEY TO HEALTH

THE JOURNEY TO HEALTH

Healing is a journey of letting go. Letting go of the myths and beliefs that limit our potential and our reality. Healing is a journey of energizing what is possible, not what is probable. It is a journey of awareness and of balancing those aspects of our life that must die so a new reality may be created, a reality of health and wholeness.

The journey to health begins with the desire for life to be different. We might begin this journey when we are awakened by a diagnosis offered to us by Western medicine, as life intervenes or as we just know that change must occur.

Healing is a journey of opening ourselves to new beliefs, new myths, and new possibilities that will bring forth new realities. On this journey, we may connect with the spirit of an illness, the spirit of a disease, or the spirit of an organ within our body to hear its voice, to find its purpose and meaning in our life.

The journey to health leads us to a world in which we may thrive, a world in which we may walk in integrity with self, with others, and with the universe. A world that is safe and in balance. Health manifests as we experience a sense of balance and well-being, an increase in self-empowerment, or just a general sense of being in which we are at peace with the events of our life.

This journey to health is not always smooth or easy. There may be bumps and dead ends along the way. There may be issues we wish not to see or acknowledge. Perhaps an unhealthy relationship, a toxic job, or limiting beliefs about who we can be in this life. Yet these issues must be seen and acknowledged for us to step into a place of health and wholeness. When we begin to see these bumps and dead ends not as obstacles but as teachers, they will challenge us to clarify our vision, to be open to new beliefs and myths, and to allow our vision of life to be dynamic.

CHAPTER ONE

WHAT IS ILLNESS?

Illness, within the Western framework of belief, may be defined as a sickness resulting from exposure to another organism or substance such as a virus, toxin, or bacteria. Illness is a time that our body is physically invaded and weakened. It is a time that our body plays host to the energy of other organisms.

In sickness, our body mobilizes its defenses to attack and defend against these intruding forces. Cells fight against cells. If our body kills more cells, we win. If the invading cells multiply quicker, they win. Western medicine typically focuses on the outside forces that have attacked us, that have created illness. The patient is cast

133

as a victim, the victim of cancer, of depression, or of an unknown illness. We have antibiotics, antifungals, and anti-inflammatories to kill and disable the invading bacteria and viruses. We mount a fight against these forces of evil. We poison the invading cells, nuke them, or perhaps cut them out. We are victorious, or we succumb to the disease in this adversarial scenario.

In the Western framework, the etiology of illness and disease focuses upon the fact that our body was invaded, that we are the victim, not upon our state of mind, our connection to Spirit, or how we may be out of harmony with the universe. In Western society we minimize, even deny, the effect of our behavior upon the state of our well-being. We do not look at our actions or behaviors as causative factors in illness. We do not take responsibility for the turmoil occurring in our life. We do not ask of ourselves, "Why was I available to this illness or event?"

The factors that we control, that create disharmony or disease, that make us susceptible to illness, have typically not been considered, as Western medicine looks at the nature or cause of illness within an individual. What if we were to examine our own life? Where might our actions be out of harmony with our self, our community, or with Spirit? How might disharmony be a causative factor in our current state of being?

The healers of the Andes say all illness, disease, and turmoil is spiritual in nature and a result of disharmony. Disharmony may be a result of conflict between our core essences and the spirits of unconscious beliefs and myths that predispose us to accept illness, disease, or turmoil into our life. We have all heard or been raised with the belief that if we go to bed with wet hair, we will be sick in the morning. Or that if we swim within an hour of eating, we will have stomach cramps and perhaps drown. Many times, as I have hiked through the Andes, I have been admonished by the Q'ero healers to immediately remove my sweat-soaked shirt as we take a moment to rest, or risk having issues with my lungs.

Through myth and belief, we invite illness and turmoil into our life. We step on a crack and our mother's back goes out the following week. We remember the voices of our mother as she admonished our behavior. We deserve to be punished, to experience disease in our life. We experience the vague symptoms of an impending illness; we expect to become ill in the circumstances we have encountered. We become ill. We stay ill, as our mind creates the thoughts and beliefs that support and justify our illness.

Yet illness may be no more than a state of being or a messenger alerting us to the fact that we are in disharmony with self, our environment, or a greater power. When we are out of right relationship, out of ayni, on any level and for any reason, we create disharmony. Disharmony may exist between our spirit and the spirits of nature, be they the spirits of the mountains or the spirits of a virus or bacteria. We may experience this disharmony as emotional or physical discomfort, or through turmoil in our life.

As individuals and communities, the healers and peoples of the Andes take responsibility for their part in creating disharmony. Then through ritual and ceremony, they create balance and harmony to make amends for their part in creating the milieu within which illness and turmoil have occurred. Once balance and harmony have been restored, they know healing may follow.

The Journey to Health Is the Responsibility of One

This journey, the journey to physical, spiritual, and emotional health on which we have embarked, is ultimately the responsibility of one individual. We are that individual. No one else is responsible for our journey. As we test the new waters of health, we may move forward slowly with baby steps or we may jump headfirst into our healed self. Whichever action we take, we leave behind an old self. An old self that was familiar and safe in knowing who we were in illness and in turmoil. An old self we no longer need, yet one we must honor.

As we proceed on this journey, we may immediately experience a sense of health and well-being or we might experience a sense of loss, of sadness, of grief, or a yearning to return to who we have been. We may choose to embody the healed state or we may choose to reengage the old ways and reclaim the unhealed state. It is important to honor the feelings that arise but not to be seduced by these feelings or by the siren calls of the one who we once were.

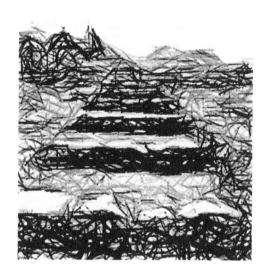

CHAPTER TWO

LEVELS OF PERCEPTION

Shamans engage the world through levels of perception. There are four levels, four realms of perception. These levels correspond to the manifestations of light and vibration which represent the physical body (the physical world), the mental/emotional (thoughts, emotions, and beliefs), the soul (myths and images), and the spiritual body (energy). A shaman may engage these realms of perception to ascertain the future and deduce the cause of illness based on a mythology greater than the literal manifestation of disease or illness.

Each perceptual level has its own language, its own frequency, and its own energetic domain. Each perceptual level is associated with a chakra and the attributes of a specific archetype of perception.

The first chakra is associated with the energy of serpent. It is the literal. The shaman perceives and describes what is. The second chakra is associated with jaguar and the energies of emotion. The shaman senses beyond the literal into the symbolic. Meaning and interpretation are given to what is. The sixth chakra brings us the gift of hummingbird and access to the mythic journey of our soul. Here a shaman may bring light and awareness as to why our soul has chosen to experience an event in this lifetime. The ninth chakra is the realm of creation where the shaman may fly with the eagle or condor into the realms of Spirit to release the energy of what has been and bring forth what may be.

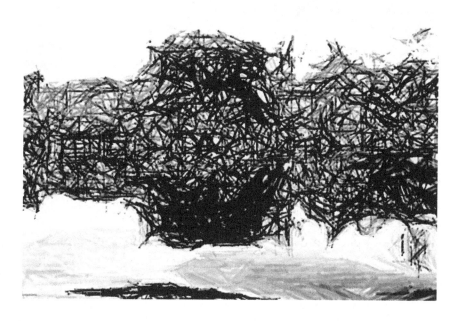

CHAPTER THREE

LENS AND FILTERS OF PERCEPTION

Within the energetic field of our body is a structure like a lens of a microscope. This lens has filters that allow us to view and interpret our universe. The filters are created by our personal experiences and beliefs and by the beliefs and experiences of our families, our culture, and our society. These filters allow us to make sense of the beliefs and the reality of the world in which we live. The lens, like the lens on the shaft of a microscope, can change position and filters so that one may see from a higher or lower perspective or through a filter that is different. Most of us never change the filter or perspective of the lens to engage life differently. Yet if we did, a whole new reality, a new world of possibility, would unfold before us.

A shaman can help us change the lens and filters through which we see and experience life. Once shifted the new perspective may allow us to engage life through new realms of being. Realms that allow us to discover ourselves in harmony, in wholeness, and in health. This is the journey of health.

On this journey of health, illness might be viewed through the perspective of the soul as an opportunity for growth and evolution. In one scenario, the soul may have agreed prior to incarnation in a physical body to experience misfortune or cancer, that it might learn compassion. While in another scenario the soul volunteered to experience death in childhood, that the souls of its parents might experience grief. Viewed from this perspective, illness and turmoil experienced in the physical realm may be a journey of health and empowerment for the soul, not a journey of victimhood. Health may be nothing more than a state of being in which the lessons learned in disease are integrated within the fabric of the soul.

In illness, in fact in all of life's events, then we are perfect as we are. We are exactly where we are meant to be to allow the soul to grow and to evolve. Were we not in that state, at that given moment, our soul could not learn or evolve.

When the soul is not able to experience or incorporate the lessons it came forth to learn, then the universe may continue to recreate events which will offer another opportunity to learn, to evolve, and to heal. At the literal perspective, we may call these opportunities chronic illness.

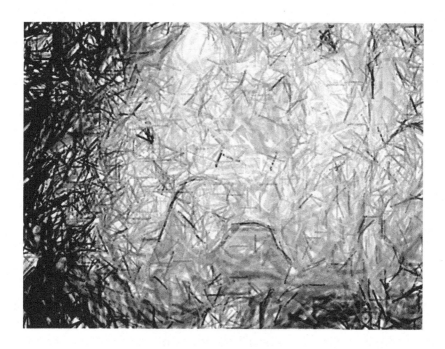

CHAPTER FOUR

TRACKING

Shamans observe. They observe without judgment, without attachment, and without entanglement in the journey of their client. They observe to diagnose the source of illness. They observe to find the archetypal maps, the myths, and the beliefs that guide a client on their journey through life.

A shaman consciously shifts and engages different filters and levels of perception to view the world of his client. As the shaman engages these different filters, he shifts his vision, his perception, to another realm—a realm that is separate from the presentation of the illness, the disease, or the presenting source of the turmoil.

This process of observation is known as tracking. As the shaman moves through the perceptual levels, energy may be seen, tasted, felt, heard, or experienced all at the same time. Tracking allows the shaman to find the energy and the voice within the energy. The shaman senses the energy to find where the energy is blocked or held in the body. Once found, and the voice of the energy heard, it can be removed and the imprints of illness, disease, and turmoil cleared.

To view illness from the literal, the shaman shifts into the perceptual level of serpent. As serpent, we evaluate the problem at an instinctual level. Here we see life, we describe life, and we experience life as it appears. We do this without emotion, judgment, or interpretation. The color red is the color red; it means nothing more. A cold is just a cold. A runny nose is just a runny nose. Life just is, as it appears.

In jaguar, nothing is as it appears to be. In jaguar, we give meaning to the everyday occurrences of our life. Meaning that is open to interpretation. In jaguar, we interpret life through the filters and eyes of our family, our culture, and our own experiences. An event is no longer described as it appears, but in jaguar becomes symbolic of life. The congestion of a cold becomes symbolic of the congestion in our daily life. The color red may symbolize good fortune, danger, or anger.

In jaguar, what may appear as chaos in our life may in fact be a finely orchestrated plan of the cosmos to assist our being twenty years from now. I now look back and see the events that have shaped my life with new understanding. Life was not what it appeared to be.

In hummingbird, everything is as it is at the moment that it is energized. A stone is a stone, but may be a musical instrument or a means of defense. It is there for us to use as we need it, in any particular moment of time. In hummingbird, illness and turmoil become a vehicle of—or a metaphor for—the soul's journey and how we are taking on the travails of life. What we are experiencing is a message for our soul. Illness may be a reminder to let go of our beliefs of what we must do in life or a reminder that we may ask for and accept help along the path of our journey.

Metaphor brings an understanding of our life told through myth and image. In metaphor, we may safely understand our own story depicted through the images and stories of another's journey through life. A shaman may see the heavy burden of a client with fatigue as the image of a man carrying boulders up a mountain. We as the observer and without judgment may then begin to release the stones and burdens we are carrying.

To release and de-energize what has been seen, the shaman releases the energy back to source. This is the perceptual level of eagle or condor. These archetypal symbols are the messengers to Spirit. The energy is released of form, interpretation, and metaphor to once again be available as the unmanifest energy of creation.

CHAPTER FIVE

PERCEPTION CREATES OUR TRUTH

A Lesson of Perception

In March 2013, what had begun as a solo pilgrimage soon grew to a group of eight souls called to the protector mountain of the Q'ero people. I was among this group of individuals who had been called by the spirit of Huaman Lipa to the high mountains of Peru. We were each called for our own reasons and for our own healing. The several-days' journey into this remote village was now a two-day hike, as foreign mining interests had begun to carve a road into the skin of Mother Earth. This remote village, protected beneath a forest of clouds from the Spaniards in the fifteenth century, would now, in a few short years, be visited once again and finally conquered by a foreign power.

As darkness approached that first night, we set up camp just shy of 16,000 feet. Soon the temperatures had dropped below freezing, and the rain that was falling turned to ice and snow. After a dinner of warm quinoa soup, we hunkered down in the apparent safety of our tents. And yet, later that night, protected from the fierce winds that were blowing outside and warmed by the wool of the alpaca blankets that covered us, we would learn how the perception or belief we hold of an experience may create safety or manifest disaster.

It was sometime around midnight that the unmistakable sounds of vomiting began from a tent nearby. The vomiting worsened and soon became dry heaves. At altitude, the immediate concern with the onset of persistent vomiting is of life-taking altitude sickness, the remedy for which is immediate descent to a lower altitude. Yet in the mountainous terrain, and under the darkness of an Andean night, this life-saving step of immediate retreat to a lower altitude was not an option.

As morning began to dawn, many of us huddled together to discuss the welfare of our companion and the possible need to curtail our pilgrimage, when suddenly, the one who vomited all night appeared and announced she had been healed. Healed of the anger, the frustration, and the guilt that she had held surrounding the death of her son, who had died unexpectedly at college. Having finally released the toxic energy, she was now ready to move forward in her life.

Symptoms of illness or manifestation of health, from the definition of Western medicine and the perspective of we who observed that night, here was a woman experiencing a life-threatening altitude event. Yet the perspective of this woman, as she repeatedly vomited throughout the night, was a mother releasing the toxins of a death that had already claimed her. This woman had not colluded with the perception of those around her. She trusted her own self, her own experience. While we viewed and judged her experience from the perceptual state of serpent, she experienced and embraced life through the eyes of hummingbird. She healed. She had been given the opportunity to live again. Today she is a powerful healer whose experience brings possibility and life to others.

Later that morning we all continued our pilgrimage to Apu Huaman Lipa. We each had responded to the call of this sacred mountain, and now we had each individually, and in community, offered our gifts and our gratitude to Mother Earth and to the spirit of this sacred being. In return, we received the blessing and wisdom of Apu Huaman Lipa.

Before leaving this great mountain several days later and returning to the lower elevations of the Sacred Valley, we were blessed by two renowned healers of the Q'ero nation, Don Sebastian and Don Mariano. Through their blessing we received the *hatun karpay*, an energetic download of initiation that brings forth gifts of great wisdom, knowledge, and power to those who are ready to receive.

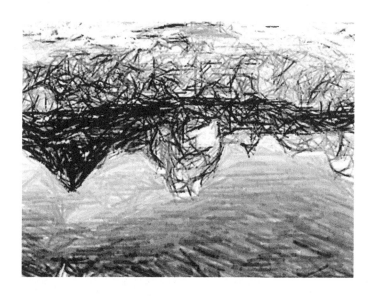

CHAPTER SIX

WHAT I PERCEIVE, I CREATE

A few weeks after returning from the journey to the high Andes, I was awakened from a deep slumber to receive a download from the spirit of Huaman Lipa.

I was told, "What I perceive in others, I am creating in my own reality. That perception affects our truths, our reality, and our interactions with others. We each have a default level of perception. The default level of perception is comfortable and known to us. This is the operating system for how we experience and make sense of the world. For some, their perception and reality is that the world is not safe, while others believe that we live in a kind and supportive universe." It was said that "there are those who experience life as it is, others whose journey is to interpret the meaning of life's experiences, and others for whom life is like a great myth or fairy tale."

In the offering of this wisdom I was told that perception is a mirror, a creation of my projection. It is the projection that creates the perception of my reality. We each have a default level of beliefs, judgments, and experiences we bring to any encounter. When we change the projection or change our perception, our truths change, our interactions change, and our reality changes.

Further I was told, "When two or more individuals come together, a vibration is created. This vibratory creation generates a unique consciousness of energy separate from, yet dependent upon, the projection and perception of each individual present. How the vibratory creation is interpreted by each of the individuals involved is dependent upon the lens and the filters each participant brings to the encounter. We create our reality through our interpretation of an event. We have projected ourselves upon the event we have encountered."

It is the projection of our beliefs and our judgment of another's action or behavior as right or wrong that creates our reality. We meet someone on the street; they greet us with a hug or kiss. Their behavior triggers a reaction within us. This reaction may be harmonious or may create unease. The vibratory creation generates a response within each of us. The response is our truth, our reality that is independent of the greeter's intent.

In one instance, this hug or kiss on the cheek might represent a greeting, just that, and nothing more. In another moment, this same action may be interpreted as an intrusion into our energetic space or even cause activation of a latent imprint surrounding intimacy. And yet at another time, this action may be received and interpreted as an invitation to romance and mystery.

The archetypal perspectives of serpent, jaguar, and hummingbird each influence how we respond to events in life. One level of perception is not better than another, just different.

Each provides an opportunity for growth and balance. Disharmony and misunderstandings can occur, however, when two individuals come together holding different levels of perception as they experience a singular event. When one participant is holding and experiencing an encounter from the perspective of hummingbird and the other in jaguar, disharmony and turmoil may be the result.

One can imagine as the romantic journeyer in hummingbird unintentionally meets the jaguar, who is defending her personal space, or as the greeter in serpent gets more than she bargained for as she meets the romantic journeyer. We each have a default level of perception from which we view and experience life. These levels of perception need not be in opposition to one another; they are just different. Each carries a gift, and it behooves us to cultivate the ability to consciously switch between these filters of perception that we may experience life in its fullest spectrum of being.

Shadow Is Like the Dark Side of the Moon

I was later told by the spirits of the mountain that we fear the darkness of our shadow. Our shadow is the part of our self that we do not see, that perhaps we wish not to see. The shadow is like the dark side of the moon. We may not see the dark side of the moon, but just as the oceans and tides are influenced by the entirety of the moon, our perception of life is influenced by the entirety of our being, including the shadow pieces of our self and soul.

Our shadow is that hidden part of us that fears, in fact knows, that we are unsafe because of *them*. We know *they* are different. We know *they* are a threat to our beliefs and our truths. We know that the world would be a better place without *them*. It is the projection of our shadow that *they* are the cause of all that is wrong in life. *They* make us full of anger, rage, guilt, and blame. We have never met *them*. We have never spoken to *them, those people, those democrats, those republicans, those gays, those rednecks* . . . But *they* make us uncomfortable. *They* are the ones who threatened the status quo, the very existence of our being.

They are the ones who threaten the unconscious myths and beliefs that we have accepted as truths. The same myths and beliefs that have been created and that we have accepted as to what is right or wrong. The myths that judge who we are and tell us who we can or should be, that we may not be seen and judged as deviant.

By not seeing our own shadow, we may hold a false sense of unity that protects us from recognizing the duality of our being. For it is "*they*" who make us uncomfortable, not the unconscious wholeness of our being. The unconscious wholeness of being that knows we, too, could be *them*, the ones we have been taught are evil. When we relegate this awareness to the shadow, our shadow protects us from this knowledge. It is in the darkness of this knowing that fear prevents us from seeing this side we call a shadow.

When we project these beliefs onto others to make *them* the unacceptable ones, the unlovable ones, and to make *them* the reason for our problems, then we do not need to confront our hidden beliefs and desires—beliefs and desires that may even have become a conscious yearning but that we cannot accept in ourselves. Perhaps these are beliefs or behaviors that we have learned from family or culture are considered unacceptable or taboo.

When we cast these beliefs and judgments out upon others, then we need not confront our desires or our feelings of compassion and love toward those who are different. We can instead live in safety knowing that wherever we look, our beliefs and our truths that *they* are bad, *they* are evil, and that *they* are the cause of all our problems will be validated through our shadow and its projections.

The spirits of the mountains also said to me that when we recognize the influence of our shadow, when we have shined light upon our unconscious and owned the projections of our shadow, we may experience the beauty and wholeness of our being. It is in this state of wholeness and beauty that we may experience acceptance and compassion of self and for all. No longer do we find the need to vilify others for our ignorance or for our soul's desires.

CHAPTER SEVEN

LIMITING BELIEFS

On this journey of health, we may be confronted and challenged by the beliefs that we hold. We may have adopted beliefs and myths that hinder our process of healing or growth. These beliefs are called limiting.

A limiting belief is just that—a belief that limits. Limiting beliefs stop us from stepping forward into our destiny and from claiming the fruits of our dreams. They prevent us from breaking free of ancestral patterns or cultural influence. A limiting belief prevents us from silencing the inner voice that says, "I cannot change . . ." "I am not worthy of . . ." or "No one could ever love me." Limiting beliefs tell us that we cannot heal. We cannot change who we are. We cannot have what we desire.

Limiting beliefs may be of our own creation, our society, or even our culture. Limiting beliefs may manifest a reality we wish not to accept, yet we do. These beliefs are powerful. We unquestionably allow the myths of these beliefs to manifest and create our reality. We are given a diagnosis. Attached to the diagnosis is the myth of the disease.

We hear the diagnosis of cancer and we accept the belief that suffering, or death, is our destiny, our fate. What if we did not accept the diagnosis given to us? What if we questioned the beliefs? What if we looked for alternate possibilities, alternate myths? What then would be our fate, our destiny? I did not accept the destiny Western medicine offered to me. Had I accepted this belief, where might I be today?

Roles and the Limiting Beliefs That Support Them

Limiting beliefs support and are generated by the roles we have taken on in life. Roles are the unconscious scripts written by society, family, and ourselves that support the myths and beliefs of who we are. Roles dictate how we must be or act in this life, how we are seen by others, and how we have internalized the expectations of our parents, our culture, or our society. We may become trapped or limited by the definition of these roles. The roles begin to create the myths and beliefs of our reality.

Common roles include mother, father, son, daughter, professional, blue-collar worker, lower class, upper class, victim, rescuer, student, caretaker, born under the astrological sign of ... etc. Attached to these roles may be judgments and labels such as devoted, absent, incorrigible, shy, poor, etc. These are the judgments and beliefs that define and limit who we can be: "He is only a blue-collar worker" (implied: he will never amount to anything more). "She is so devoted to her children" (implied: she will never put herself first). "He is only a 'B' student" (implied: he can never get an "A"). "I am a diabetic." "I am a victim of cancer, or of . . ."

The good child, or the bad child of the family. Each role has an expectation and fate attached to it. When we identify with a role, we become defined by the beliefs and by the judgments that the role carries. When we identify ourselves in a role such as the victim, we begin to believe that is who we are and become trapped and limited by this archetypal image. Our beliefs, myths, and reality take on the energy of the victim. Our identity becomes vested in this role.

We not only act the victim; we accept the fate and the destiny of the victim. Unconsciously we ask others to see us as we now see ourselves in this role that has been created, the role of the victim. Our friends, family, and society believe this is who we are; in their eyes we have become the victim. They judge us, hold us to the expectation and fate this role has created, even if that expectation is death. When we do not meet the expectation the role carries, our friends and family label us as a deviant or perhaps a troublemaker. We are failures in the eyes of their expectation. We are the victim.

Roles carry the beliefs of the masses. As individuals we may accept, without thought, how roles are defined by others and allow them to become binding and limiting truths in our own lives. Yet these truths may be the truths and judgments of another that, if one wishes to accept, will limit who we may become. When we listen to the callings of our soul, we know that what might be right for the masses is not nourishing for us. Many believe that a mother must be fully devoted to her family, that she must give up or suspend her dreams of being a physician, a minister, or an artist as she embraces the role of motherhood.

To heal, first we must identify the roles we have accepted. Next we must observe these roles and how they define who we are. Finally, we must release how the voices of family, culture, and society live within these roles, the truths that we have embodied and now limit who we may become. Releasing our roles means we are no longer defined only by the role as a mother or as a child. Roles are dynamic. We will always be a mother, a son, but the mother we are to our son who is three months old, sixteen years old, and thirty-five years old is different.

We, too, must be dynamic in how we hold these roles. We must release who we are, who we were, to evolve into who we are becoming or who we wish to be. Through ritual, ceremony, and awareness, we may transform how we carry these roles. The roles then become something we can either choose to be and do, or not. We know that along with being a mother or son, we may also be an artist, a physician, or a minister, and yet not be defined by those roles either.

Once the roles and expectations we carry have been released, we are free to embody who we are becoming. We can begin to create our own myth and to write our own story, a story authored by us, a story that will empower us, and a story that will allow us to break free of the beliefs and judgments of others. We create this myth from the eyes of the observer—free from the confines of the beliefs, reality, and myths of others we may envision the image of who we wish to be.

When we have released and honored who we have been, we are free to connect to the power of the healed or whole self. We are free to create our own reality, beliefs, and myths that are not predicated upon who we are, who we have been, or who others think we should be or by what they have experienced. It is these new myths of creation that will pull us forward to the reality we desire to live, to create, and to be part of. In this process we may release the outdated contracts of our soul—contracts that once served us but that now limit our growth and evolution as spiritual beings.

When we have released ourselves from the myths and beliefs of others, we are then free to experience life through the lenses and filters that we choose to create. These may be filters that reveal the beauty and abundance of life. Or perhaps filters that allow us to experience a life of wholeness, health, and balance. The choice will be ours and nourished by the myths and beliefs that we create to guide us through life.

CHAPTER EIGHT

BELIEFS, MYTH, AND REALITY

Thoughts and Beliefs Create

Whatever beliefs we hold consciously or unconsciously, the universe will mirror them back to us to create our reality. Thoughts, judgments, and words are energy—energy with a vibratory signature attached that may create change in what already is or may manifest anew in our reality.

Most of us are aware of Doctor Emoto's experiment with thought, form, and water. Doctor Emoto showed with the aid of microscopy that thought affected the molecular structure of water. High vibrational thoughts created beauty and harmony in the molecular structure of water. Low vibrational thoughts created disharmony in these same molecules. High vibrational thoughts are of love and joy. Low vibrational thoughts are of anger, shame, doubt, and hate.

Much of what we in the Western classifications of life consider alive—such as plants, animals, and bacterial organisms—is composed of large percentages of water. Indeed, the human body is 70 percent water. How might the vibration of our own thoughts and beliefs, or the thoughts and beliefs of others, affect life as we know it?

Practitioners of Chinese medicine are aware that emotions turned inward create disease. When our thoughts, either self-directed or directed at the sources of our nourishment, are of anger, hatred, or discordance, the universe may manifest anger, hatred, or discordance within or toward us. We hold a negative body image. We are angry at our thighs, our breasts, or the monthly cycle. Perhaps we bring the heavy emotions of the day to the meal we are preparing, or we are angry at this food because it makes us fat. When these heavy energies are the nourishment and vibrations we feed our body, they may create disharmony and chaos within our being. This disharmony may later manifest as illness or disease.

Metaphorically, how often do we stand at the mouth of a canyon and yell, *I hate you, you are fat, you are ugly, you are worthless*, or a myriad of other thoughts and beliefs about ourselves? The canyon echoes our words back to us tenfold until they are just whispers unconsciously creating our life. It is these whispers, the softest whispers in the jungle of our unconsciousness, that become the loudest voices of the universe.

When did we last stand at the mouth of the canyon and yell, *I am joy, I am beauty, I am love*, and hear these words echo back? Each breath, each inhalation is a chance to observe, to be aware, and to grow. Awareness allows us to transform our thoughts before the energy of our thoughts and beliefs manifests into reality. Tonight, as we face the canyons of our unconscious, let us allow joy, beauty, and love to be the echoes and the whispers of the canyons that inform who we are and become the manifestations of the universe we create.

Myths Inform Our Beliefs

Our myths, our judgment of what is success, of what is right or wrong, and our myths of who we are or who we ought to be create our reality. When others create these myths, then we live in a reality that is not ours.

One night, while deep in ceremony in the jungle outside of Iquitos, I strayed into the mirage of an opium den. I found myself shrouded in the smoke of the pipes, intermingled with dreams and nightmares, floating within visions and realities that were not mine. Then there was a voice: "Stay out of their dreams. Do not accept the dreams of others. They are not yours." Years earlier I was admonished by the voice of San Pedro, "If you do not wish to be here, in this situation, then you need not be."

I could have stayed, lost myself and my reality that night, but the dreams, the reality, were not mine. I did not wish to be here, in this realm of reality. Then I heard again, "Do not accept other people's dreams. Stay out of their dreams." This realm of reality, its myths and beliefs, was not mine. I instead chose to be somewhere different, to create my own dream of reality.

We have the right to dream our own existence, our own reality, our own self into being. We have the right to create and change our reality. We change our reality not by changing our beliefs, but by changing the myth that created the beliefs that created our reality.

When we observe without judgment, without attachment, then the myths we have lived and are living can be retold to create a new reality. A reality in which we can just be; others can just be. Our energy can then be directed toward creation of our own reality, not as others want us to be or what they perceive we need to make them comfortable in their reality.

It follows as well that we must avoid dreaming the life of others into being. For it is their spirit's path, their soul's path and mandate to dream, to grow, and to create their own reality, not ours to do so for them.

CHAPTER NINE

MYTHS AND GODS

Our myths support our gods and our world vision. Myths inform our beliefs. Beliefs that inform, that create our reality, our world vision, and the gods we worship. When our myths and gods serve us, they protect us. They empower us. They allow us to exist in harmony with our vision of reality.

Reality is our truth, our perception of life as we interpret it. Reality and beliefs are influenced by the life experiences, the beliefs, and the myths that we have been exposed to through family, culture, and heredity. My reality of life or of an event in life is based upon my experiences and may be different than yours. This is not good or bad; it just is. Myths create our beliefs and reality. They create and feed the gods we serve.

In Western society, our gods are of materialism, of suffering, of lack, and of emotion. These gods ask that we create a myth, a myth that if we worship them, they will turn the lead of our life into gold. These are the gods of greed, fear, money, guilt, suffering, lack, doubt, technology, attachment, judgment, etc. These gods are the alchemists of Western society.

They are false gods. They are false alchemists. They ask that we create a myth and a reality where we suffer for lack of obtaining what they offer us, that we are defective, that we are lacking without their latest product. These are the gods we serve in Western culture. These are the gods with whom we strive to be in ayni. The gods who promise to turn our life, our reality, into gold if only we worship them. The ones who create a world in which we are defective, incomplete, and victims without their gifts. Gods that Madison Avenue has created. Gods that support our fears, our greed, our perceived need for the newest electronic gadget or item of clothing. Gods that ask we devote our life energy to obtaining the gold they offer us so that they may be fed.

They say that in return for our loyalty, our need to consume, and our reliance upon their myths and beliefs, we will be happy. They say we will be given a life of joy and beauty, a life of wholeness and health, a life in which we are in ayni with all that is. This is their promise and the belief they create for us.

But what are we giving up? What are the limitations of the reality we choose to accept to obtain their promises? How have these gods and their myths limited our lives? What do we fear? What are the myths, beliefs, or emotions that hold us in fear of what we lack? Who or what has created this fear within us? How do we allow fear or perceptions of scarcity to create our life?

When we feel no better, when our gods no longer serve us, we create new gods—gods who will create new myths, new beliefs, and new realities that will serve us. These gods will become the ones we worship as we rush out to buy their latest offerings—offerings they claim will create gold for us. And we will worship these gods, and they will serve us, until they no longer do.

Let us take this moment to ask: Who are our gods? Who has created these gods? How do they serve us? What myths and beliefs have they created to influence our choices and create our reality? Are they gods that ask us to live in a world of anger to avoid intimacy and compassion? Do they want us to live in a world of hate to avoid the uncertainty and vulnerability of love? Do they ask that we hold onto the myth of scarcity to avoid the loss of abundance? Perhaps we may need ask, "Are these the gods that serve and support the reality of our desire and creation?"

CHAPTER TEN

THE HUMAN BRAIN

The human brain is composed of four levels. Each level has its own function and language. The two most primitive levels of the brain deal with scarcity and survival. The responses and actions of these primitive levels are instinctual. These are levels where toxic emotions may imprison us, where anger and fear may paralyze or consume us. At these levels of the brain, we may sabotage our own healing.

This act of sabotage may be due to a fear of change, of achieving wholeness, or even a fear of who we can become. At the literal, we may fear losing our role and our identity of being ill, of being a victim, or of being disabled. Our mind and ego may even fear being abandoned by our caretaker, our spouse, or our healer if we become well. We become our worst and most powerful enemy. Yet our ego, our mind, denies we are doing this, as time and time again we unconsciously call back the behavior, the belief system, or the energy of the imprint we desire to heal.

In shamanic belief, this unconscious behavior of calling back the undesired behavior is an act of self-sorcery. Sorcery is harm directed against another or against oneself. A sorcerer is someone whose action intentionally or unintentionally creates an imbalance in the energy field which may lead to physical illness or psychological dysfunction.

Sorcery can be either external (another individual) or from an internal source (our self). Either way, sorcery affects the primitive brains. When these sub-brains are reactive and out of balance, operating in a state of disequilibrium, our thoughts and actions may become irrational. This can result in both physical and emotional suffering.

Sorcery may be conscious or unconscious. Conscious sorcery occurs when we intentionally direct disharmony toward another individual. Unconscious sorcery occurs when we gossip, hold anger, or think disempowering thoughts about ourselves or others. In fact, the power of our thoughts and beliefs, be they unconscious or even subconscious, can create imbalance in an individual's energy field, even if there is no intent to create harm.

We are most susceptible to sorcery when fear lives within us. Fear-based beliefs and imprints are activated by anger, disharmony, and doubt. Once activated fear feeds upon itself, paralyzing and depleting the vital energy of the body.

For one to override the survival instincts and heal the wounds of the two primitive levels, one must work with the higher levels of the brain. The levels that may dream, create, and speak to the myths of the soul. These are the levels where we work with the mythic, with the arts, with creativity, and where we may connect with the higher aspects of our being. These are the levels where we may create rituals and ceremony that may transform the beliefs and transmute the fear or other emotions that have imprisoned us. These are the levels where we may create new myths and beliefs to create a new reality.

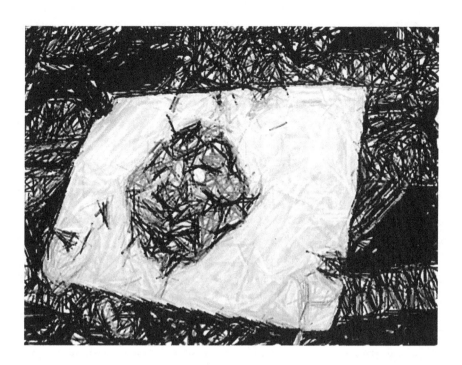

CHAPTER ELEVEN

CEREMONY

Ceremony is an integral part of shamanic healing. Ceremony creates a means to honor and release the myths, the gods, the beliefs, and the reality we have been living. Ceremony overrides the survival instincts of the primitive brain, allowing us to let die that which must so we may create new life. Ceremony allows energy to be transformed and the myths and beliefs that support turmoil to be transcended

Each time we open our mesa, work with our *khuyas* (sacred stones), or work with a client, we step into ceremony. We create sacred space. We set our intent for healing. Energy is transformed and released to spirit. We transcend who we were and who we are, to create who we will become. We close sacred space. The transformation is complete.

Ceremony is composed of rites and rituals. Rituals are structured actions that create the vessel and hold the ceremony. The act of chanting, the use of a rattle, the donning of ceremonial clothing are examples of ritual. Rites are the intent and the focus of a ceremony. Rites facilitate movement, passage, and transformation for an individual. The rite of ceremony may be transformation, initiation, or the honoring of what has been.

In ceremony, the dynamic and spontaneous intervention of Spirit may manifest to create transformation and transcendence. Through ceremony, we create a vessel in which our intent is held and offered to the universe, yet it is Spirit who manifests the intention, the change.

In ceremony, at the place of the mythic, the literal can be transformed into pure energy. This pure energy is the unmanifest energy of creation, of all possibility that can create health, harmony, wholeness, beauty, joy, balance, and love. This pure energy is the energy of the void, the place before creation. We can then take this pure energy back into our body to create our new being, our new becoming in life. In ceremony, we call forth the spirits of nature and the spirits of the waters, wind, earth, and fire to catalyze and assist in the process of change.

Ceremony allows for creation and manifestation of the intent to occur. While the intent of the rite directs what may unfold in ceremony, how the intention manifests is unique to each participant. No ceremony is the same. In fact, when two or more individuals participate in the same ceremony, the experience of the ceremony is unique and dynamic for each.

Ceremony speaks to the soul of our being. The language of the soul and of the mythic is found in poems, fairy tales, songs, and images. As these energies are brought together in ceremony, we may release blockages, create new paths, and bring forth new myths of empowerment.

Ceremonies have three parts in their structure: the beginning, the middle, and the ending. In shamanic ceremony, the beginning may be signified by the creation of sacred space. This is the sacred vessel in which ceremony will occur. Let's use fire as the ceremony and transformation as the rite to provide an example of ceremony.

We set our intention for ceremony. The intention for the fire ceremony is transformation. We collect the sticks and lay a fire in which to transform that which we desire to change. We open sacred space. We call upon the archetypal energies and healers of the universe to be present. We ask that they share their medicine and gifts of healing. We might sanctify and cleanse the space and the participants with sage or sacred waters. By these acts we are shifting our awareness to the mythic and to the level of the soul. We have created the vessel. This is the beginning.

The middle part of ceremony occurs with the unfolding and manifestation of the intention for the ceremony. This is the place where the intention transforms into the intended, the manifestation rather than the desire. We remember the fire ceremony is one of transformation. We begin to chant, to light the transformational fire. We bless and feed the fire.

We offer our thanks as we blow our gratitude to that which we are ready to release into a stick. We kneel before the fire. We offer the stick that now represents that which we are honoring and releasing to the fire. We call upon the spirit of the fire to receive our offering and to transform this energy back to pure light. This light is now available to feed or guide us on the next part of our journey.

We have blown our individual intention and prayers into the stick. The intention of the ceremony has been declared for each individually. Here in the middle portion of ceremony, the stick that we bring to a fire is no longer a stick but becomes the carrier of what must die within us so the new may be born. What must die is then placed into the fire to be transformed.

It is here that our intention manifests into the intended. The transformation is complete. Fire transformed the literal and emotional back into the energetic. From the energetic, from all that is possible, we can create our new being. Our intention has now manifested into the intended.

In this ceremony, we come to the fire with intention, desire, and purpose. We chant around the fire. This is ritual. The chanting is not the intention of the ceremony. The chanting is the structure, the ritual that allows us to bypass the thinking mind. The fire releases and transforms the energy that was once bound within us into light. This light is then brought back into our energy centers so what once was bound within us is now available as light to feed and nourish our body and luminous field as we create a new vision and dream of who we are.

Symbolically, the wind (our breath) carries the energy that is bound within out of the body and into the stick. Once this energy is blown into the stick, the stick is no longer a stick. It is the emotion or the belief to be transformed. The fire then releases this energy contained in the stick and transforms the energy into pure light. What was once bound within us, blocking our journey, has been removed, transformed. The light is now available to feed, nourish, and guide us along our path. It is this light, this energy that is brought into the three main energy centers of the body: the belly, the heart, and the forehead. This energy is the energy of creation and all possibility.

To end this ceremony, we give thanks to the spirits and healers who have assisted us during the ceremony and release them back to nature and the universe. The sacred vessel is released. The ceremony is closed.

Ceremony may create an opportunity to release judgment, practice forgiveness, and energize compassion. In place of a fire, we might blow our honoring into a flower and release this flower into a stream, watching as it floats away. We may create any form of ceremony that speaks to the essence of who we are, as we ready ourselves to transform and transcend our being. What are the myths, the beliefs that are ready to be released in your life?

Chapter Twelve

Sacred Space

Shamans work within sacred space. Sacred space is high vibrational energy concentrated within a vessel of containment. In the Andean cosmology, these areas are called *huacas.* A huaca occurs spontaneously in nature. This high vibrational energy may be found at the source of a spring, the mouth of a cave, the coming together of two rivers, in a boulder, in a sacred place, or in an object. Our mesas and sacred altars are vessels of this energy. Many churches and temples have been built around or atop these fields of energy.

Through awareness and with our intent, each time we open sacred space to bring forth the healing energies of the cosmos, we create a huaca. In the opening of sacred space, we are not creating sacred energy, for all energy is sacred. We are bringing our awareness to this energy and creating a space in which it may be held and concentrated, allowing healing and balance to occur.

To create sacred space, we call forth in reverence the power and the energy of the cosmos. We bring awareness to, and acknowledge the existence (past, present, and future) of our sacred brothers and sisters, in all realms, and in all forms. We invite our ancestors and our teachers to join in with us. We invite the spirits of the land and of the fire. We invite the spirits of the elements, the stars, the mountains, the waters, and all the lineage of healers to be present and to create this vessel of healing, this huaca. In this process, we are bringing awareness to the sacred energy that exists around us and creating a vessel in which to hold this energy.

The invocation found below may be used to bring your awareness to this sacred energy. Use this, if you please, to create your own healing space. It is my adaptation of the invocation offered and generously shared by Alberto Villoldo.

I would recommend opening sacred space as one reads and processes the exercises in this book.

Invocation

To begin, turn toward the direction that is being addressed and recite the appropriate paragraph. When ready to close the space, thank and release the directions, Mother Earth, and Father Sun.

To the winds of the South, great serpent
Wrap your coils of light around us
Teach us to shed our past, as you shed your skin
We thank you for your gifts of wisdom, of knowledge, of healing, and
of fertility in all that we undertake.

To the winds of the West, mother sister jaguar, Otorongo
Come, come and protect our medicine space
Bring us the strength and the courage to walk this path
Teach us to walk in peace and with impeccability
Allow us to see what must die both within and outside so that the
new may be born.

To the winds of the North, siwar Q'enti hummingbird, grandmothers, grandfathers, ancient ones, come and warm your hands by our fire, whisper to us in the wind.

We honor those who have come before us and those who will come after, our children's children.

We thank you for your gifts of growth and evolution. We thank you as our soul reconnects with the songs of the cosmos and we remember our sacred journey.

To the winds of the East, great eagle, condor
You who have come from the place of the rising sun,
Who brings forth the newness of each day, and the energies of possibility.

You, who have taken us under your wings to teach us to fly wingtip to wingtip with Spirit. And have allowed us to soar above ourselves, to see with great vision and breath. We thank you. We thank you for your gifts of vision, clarity, foresight, transformation, and Transcendence.

Mother Earth, we come for the healing of all. The stone people, the plant people, the four-legged, the two-legged, the finned, the furred, the creepy crawlers, all of creation and all of your children.

We thank you for this vessel, this foundation you have created to allow us to journey this path of life.

Father Sun, Inti Taita, Grandmother Moon, Mama Killa, star nations, star brothers, star sisters, yapan chaskakuna, yapan apukuna, Apu Ausangate, Apu Salkantay, Apu Huamalipa, Apu Whitney, all the sacred mountains come, come and be with us. Healers of all lineages. Mamma Coccha, mother of the Waters, Creator, Creatrix, you who are of one energy, great Spirit, thank you for allowing us to be here as we walk once again as one.

CHAPTER THIRTEEN

FATE VS. DESTINY

Fate

The journey through life and the experiences we encounter on this journey are often described as fate. Many believe fate is immutable, that it is written in the stars, cast upon us before we are born into this life. Some believe we are born into life to atone for misdeeds of the past, or to experience the healing of traumas we have previously suffered.

Many believe the fate of life is predetermined. It might be said of an individual, "He was born into this life to experience greatness, to serve, or to experience suffering." We might even refer to the circumstances of an event as "This was fated to be."

Fate may carry us through life like the waters of a river. Waters that spring forth from the source and flow aimlessly through the countryside till they reach the ocean. In these waters is a current that carries the jetsam of life. Fate may be like this river as it courses through the countryside of our life, encountering what it will along the way. In the waters of our life, this current may be engaged with awareness or accepted without question.

When we blindly accept the waters of our life as they are, we encounter what is probable in this river of life. When these waters are filled with love and joy or peace and tranquility, it may be a wonderful journey. But what if the current that carries us and the waters that feed us are filled with the probability of illness, disease, or turmoil?

Well, if we are to believe that fate and our journey through life are fixed, then we may suffer. But what if our fate is transmutable, and the course of our journey changeable? What then? Well then, as the shamans know, we can change our fate.

The probable outcomes of life are the products of our myths and beliefs, and of our life experiences. These factors may include the wounds we have not healed, the influences of our ancestors, or the genetic expression of our inheritance. Through the conscious engagement of these factors, we may chart our course and navigate the rivers of life. We may call forth our destiny.

Destiny allows us to participate in the journey of life. When we practice awareness and exercise choice, we may release the jetsam of what is probable and transform *what is* into *what can be*. When we consciously engage the currents and the waters that carry us through life, we may choose to be in a river full of possibility rather than one limited by probability. We may cast into the river of life and anchor a hook into our desired future.

As we retrieve our cast, we bring forth into the present, into the current of our life, the energized manifestation of our desire. We no longer need to search for happiness, for as we bring happiness into the current of our life, the imagined materializes. What we had desired, what others had called improbable, now manifests. We are happiness.

We wish our journey through life to reflect the journey our soul came forth to experience. This may be the journey we have been fated or the journey that manifests through awareness and self-discovery. This journey of our soul may be one of toil and hardship or a journey of joy and beauty. Whatever the mystery of this journey our soul has come forth to experience, we wish it to be ours, not a journey created by the needs or baggage of another.

Remember, with each breath, each thought, and each action we take, we may manifest our destiny into the here and now. While the ultimate destination of our life may be the same for destiny as for fate, destiny allows us to consciously call forth and to choose the current we ride through life.

CHAPTER FOURTEEN

MOMENTUM

In the last chapter we spoke of fate as the preordained course of a river that we travel when we live unconsciously—a river whose power and force carry us blindly through life. When we live unconsciously, we may dive unthinkingly into this river and be swept by the momentum of its currents into a life we would not choose and feel we cannot stop. It is the power and force of this river that creates our future as it carries us through life.

Momentum is the power and force inherent to an object that is in motion. The momentum of an object is dependent upon the mass and velocity of that object while it is in motion. If the mass or the velocity of the object increases while in motion, then the momentum of the object will increase. Conversely, if the mass or velocity of this object decreases while in motion, then the power and force of the object's momentum will decrease. The greater the momentum, the harder it becomes to stop the forward motion of an object. With life it is the same.

The momentum of our life begins to gather even before we are born into this lifetime and will continue to flow after we die to this world. We are carried by this momentum through the rivers of life into a future created by the mass and velocity of the myths and beliefs that create our reality. There are no dams to slow the speed or reduce the power of this river. And just as the banks of a river can be rigid and funnel the power and force of its current straight ahead, our lens of life may be rigid and unyielding. We are kept from seeing alternatives as we are pushed by the momentum of life into a future reality that we may not desire.

The velocity of our life is the result of the pace at which we live; the number of cups of coffee we need each day, the number of hours we spend on the smartphone or in front of the computer, watching and reliving, again and again, the tragedies of the day. Frozen in front of the twenty-four-hour news feeds, being told what might happen to us or our country if we are not hypervigilant, we are held captive by the rush of adrenaline that feeds our fight-or-flight response.

The mass of our life is composed of the baggage we carry. The weight of this baggage is a collection of the beliefs, the roles, the myths, the woundings, and the stories that we or others have created and we carry.

We are pushed into our future reality based on the mass of these myths and beliefs and by the speed at which we live—a reality that is influenced by our life experiences and by our myths of creation. We can only access the possibilities of life when we shift our beliefs and myths, when we release the stories of suffering and victimhood, and as we live with awareness and in stillness.

CHAPTER FIFTEEN

AWARENESS AND CHOICE

Awareness

Awareness and free will are key factors that support our journey to health and well-being. When we have awareness, we have choices: to consume the nutrients that support the expression of health, to release and transform the emotions that consume us, and to surround ourselves in an environment that promotes peace and wellness.

Epigenetics is the study of how genes are regulated by our environment. Science has found that the foods we eat regulate our genes by turning on and off the expression of health. It has also demonstrated that stress, emotions, and our thoughts affect the expression of those genes that bring forth health.

As we shift our beliefs, our stories, and the expression of our genes, we can shift the course of the river so the flow of the current leading to the *possible* aligns as the *probable*. As the possible transforms into the probable, what was possible now manifests as our reality. We create a life of empowerment, a life we may live in joy and beauty, in abundance and balance, in health and wholeness, and in love and light.

When we live in awareness, we see our part in the creation of life. We remember that we may cast into the lake of possibilities and reel in the essences of joy and beauty, of abundance and balance, and of wholeness and health. We may have what we desire.

When we live in awareness, we remember that our thoughts, words, and actions, both inward and outward, affect our life and the world in which we live. We know that when we release the disempowering stories, the limiting beliefs, and the attachment to suffering and victimhood, we can create a new life story that feeds a new reality, a reality of joy and beauty, a reality of wholeness and health. We know as we take time to nourish our self and our soul, we may experience the essence of love and light.

Choice

As soon as we become aware, we have choices. We have the choice to be who we desire. We have the choice to be the victim of illness or to heal. We have the choice to continue the same actions, patterns, and beliefs that have created the illness, disease, or turmoil in our life. We have the choice to create new actions, patterns, and beliefs that promote health, balance, and harmony in our life.

We may turn off the television. We may reduce the caffeine, we may walk in nature, or we may sit in meditation. We have the choice to hold on to anger, fear, and hatred, or we have the choice to welcome joy, beauty, compassion, and love into our life. We have the choice to suffer or we have the choice to create a new empowering story. We have the choice to live this new story or continue to live a story that creates illness, turmoil, and disease.

The Wolves We Feed

Let us take a moment to read and reflect on this often-told story of an Elder who is teaching his grandson about life.

The Elder says to his grandson, "A fight is going on inside me. It is between two wolves. One wolf is evil; he thrives on anger, envy, sorrow, regret, greed, arrogance, self-pity, guilt, resentment, inferiority, lies, false pride, superiority, and ego." He continued, "The other wolf is good; he thrives on joy, peace, love, hope, serenity, health, humility, kindness, benevolence, empathy, generosity, truth, compassion, and faith."

The grandson thought about it for a minute and then asked his grandfather, "Which wolf will win?"

The Elder simply replied, "The one I feed."

These wolves live within each of us. These wolves influence our actions, presence, and reality in this life. Let us take a moment to ask this question of ourselves: "Which wolf am I feeding, the wolf that thrives on fear and anger, or the wolf that thrives on love, compassion, and courage?" If the answer is fear and anger, we might ask how living in fear or with anger serves us. Or perhaps we may ask, "When I source from fear or anger, how or from what am I protected? How are my myths and beliefs validated?"

The Roles That Define Us

Roles that we choose to create or roles that we accept contribute to the mass that feeds the momentum of our life. Roles define who we are as individuals, and as a society or culture. Roles dictate how we must act or be, how we are seen by others, and how we will internalize the expectations of our parents, our culture, or our society.

When we choose to participate in the journey of our life, when we choose to reduce the momentum of our life, we may release the roles, the labels, and the judgments that have defined who we are. These roles and expectations are the weight and the baggage that have propelled us forward into what is probable, not possible in life. When we choose to disidentify with the roles we have carried, we shed the limiting beliefs and the stories they have supported. This act of disidentification will allow us to redefine who we are.

In this process of redefinition, we remove the energy of the beliefs and judgments that have trapped us in familial, cultural, and societal expectations and patterns. We release the paradigms that have held us back from exploring who we are or who we might become. We become free to choose and explore the roles we desire.

***** Exercise*****

Let us find a quiet spot where we will not be disturbed. Then through the eyes of the observer, let us make a list of the roles that define who we are. These are the roles and beliefs that we have created for ourselves or have accepted from others. There is no judgment, just an acknowledgment and an awareness of the energies we carry.

For each of the roles we have identified, let us become aware of how the role lives within us. As we consciously bring forth into our awareness a role we have identified, we ask how the energy is held in our body. Where do we instinctively know the role lives within us? Where do we sense limitation in our body or in our life? Where do we sense discomfort? Do we experience heaviness or tightness in our body? How do we stand, how do we sit as we become aware of each of these roles? Does the role elicit a strong emotion, a thought, or a judgment that may need to be transformed in ceremony? If so, blow this response into a stone or take the issue that has aroused the response to a fire.

Now let us direct our breath to the areas of tightness or discomfort we have identified for each role. With awareness and intent, we will use our breath to release this energy from our body. We will do this in ceremony. We set our intent to release these energies from our energetic field. We open sacred space. With each role we will blow the role, the beliefs, the expectations, and the judgments associated with this role into a stick. It may take one breath or more than twenty-five breaths to fully release the role and the associated beliefs from our body and into the stick. There may be threads of beliefs and supporting roles that reach back to our parents or grandparents. We will take the stick, and with a counterclockwise motion, just like rolling string onto a stick, unravel these threads from our body. We make a fire—it may be as simple as a candle—to transform and transmute this energy once again into the pure light of creation.

As the fire begins to burn, let us take a moment to honor the beliefs and roles we have carried, for they have created who we are today. Then in ceremony, we ask the spirit of the fire to transform the energy of these beliefs and roles into pure light. We place the sticks into the flame and watch as the roles we have released are consumed by the fire, as they are transformed into light. We repeat this process for each role, each label, and each judgment we have carried. We sit by the fire until we see the energies totally released of form.

When we have completed burning the roles, labels, and judgments, we bring our hand through the light of the fire. We bring this light into our belly, our heart, and our forehead to feed and nourish the energy centers of the body. As we perform this process, we may use the light of this fire to shine light into the darkness of our shadow. We may observe how each role has lived within us, and how now we are free of this role as it has defined and limited who we have been.

Symbolically and in ceremony, we release how the voices and expectations of ourselves, our family, our culture, and our society live within us and unconsciously shape our life. The roles and the associated beliefs and judgments are transformed by the flames of the fire into pure light. This light is now available to feed and nourish our body and soul as we create a new vision and dream of who we are.

We Change Because We Desire Change

When we are not reacting, when we are no longer chased or haunted by an experience, when there is no attachment to what is or what is not, we can change. We can say, "I have lived life in fear and in scarcity, and now I choose to experience certainty and abundance."

We change because we desire to change, not because others desire us to change. Remember, when we are living someone else's myths or beliefs or when we change to please another, then we are living in their reality, not ours. "They" are creating our life.

When we practice awareness, we may observe our thoughts and beliefs, both conscious and unconscious. When we have both awareness and acceptance, we may consciously shift and transform the circumstances of our life. It is through awareness that we may reduce the momentum of life and begin the journey of empowerment and healing.

CHAPTER SIXTEEN

WHERE ALL IS POSSIBLE

When we journey, we step into that magical place outside of time and space, that place where all is seen, all is possible. We are an observer of life, not the victim or perpetrator in this process. Guided imagery is a powerful catalyst of healing as the visions brought forth speak to our soul and of our creation. Just the act of seeing, if only in our mind's eye, may energize, create, and manifest an outcome. When we journey, we may see the origins of our myths and beliefs.

We may see the origins of life and perhaps of the cosmos. When we journey, we may call forth and visualize the life we wish to create for ourselves and for the universe. We may view and change our destiny before it occurs. We may connect with our healed self to bring it forth in health and in balance with all that is.

The Life That We Are Living

Let us take a moment to view the life we are living. Once again let us find a spot in which we may be at peace and in harmony with our surroundings as we prepare to journey. Perhaps we find a cozy corner of a room or a spot beneath a tree outside. We allow the self to enter a place of honesty, non-judgment, and non-attachment.

When we begin this journey, we ask that our breath carry us into a beautiful meadow, a meadow full of joy, peace, and serenity. As our breath carries us into this meadow, we become aware how we are welcomed by Mother Earth. We feel her love and her embrace. We become aware of the foundation she has created to hold and receive our presence. We know she is our constant and will always be there for us. We may become aware of the flowers and the trees that grace this meadow and of the fragrances and colors they bring to us.

Perhaps there is an awareness of their healing essence as it infuses and brings peace, serenity, and harmony to our being. Perhaps we become aware of the warmth of the sun upon our skin, or the soft, gentle light of grandmother moon as she brings light to the darkness of our life. There may be the sense of touch, a caress of our body or of our hair offered by the spirit of the wind.

We become aware of a river that flows through the meadow and we remember our intention for this journey to view without judgment, and with honesty, the river of our life. To be shown the origins of our life, the myths and beliefs that have created who we are. To be shown how we have been shaped by these myths and where we will be carried into the future of our life by the beliefs and roles these myths have brought forth.

We find a comfortable place and sit along the banks of this river. We begin to observe as the essence and milestones of our life float by. At first it might be faces or thoughts that we know well; these are like the leaves of a tree that just float by, carried on the surface of the waters. As we continue to observe the currents of our life, a branch of a tree might float along, carried by the deeper currents of the river. It is these deeper currents we pay attention to, for they are the shadows, the snags, the unconscious myths and beliefs that have created our life today.

As we watch our life pass by, we observe where we are now, who we are today. We see our reality. We see this reality without judgment or attachment. We might ask and be shown whose myths, whose beliefs these are that have created the reality we are experiencing. The current of the water may carry us upstream to the beginning of these myths and beliefs. We may recognize the myths and beliefs of our parents, our culture, or our society. We may see the beliefs that we have created and how they have served us, or perhaps how they no longer serve us.

As we become aware of these beliefs and see how they support our reality, we might ask, "Is this the reality I desire?" We may then choose to honor and to release the myths and the beliefs that no longer serve us to the current of the river to be carried away.

As we sit on the banks of this river, we might begin to ask, "What reality do we wish to create instead?" And as we ask this question, we may connect with the essence of the reality we desire. It may be the essence of joy and beauty, of wholeness and health, or perhaps an essence of peace and tranquility, or of abundance and balance. The current of the river may bring to us a spirit guide or power animal to help manifest this new reality, or perhaps the current brings to us a piece of our self, or of our soul, that has been absent and that will now once again walk this journey with us.

As our breath begins to return us to this time and place, to this body, we offer our gratitude for the gifts of healing that we have received on this journey.

Intent and Intention

Awareness and desire allow us to consciously bring forth creation. Once we connect with the essence of a new reality, we may begin to see the images of this new reality take form. A form and a reality that will serve who we are now.

Intent and visualization are part of transformation and the alchemical process of creation. Intent is the life force of intention. Intent directs energy. Intention is the matrix of life. As we draw upon the life force of intent, we create, we form an intention.

Visualization energizes form. We remember an intention combined with the energy of visualization creates manifestation of the intent. The act of seeing, even if only in our mind's eye, energizes, creates, and can manifest the intent in form. Where and what energy we direct into the matrix of life is what we create. We direct fear; we create fear. We direct beauty; we create beauty within and around us.

Let us offer an example

We will create the intent to bring forth the seeds of peace. We call forth the essence of peace from the void, the unmanifest energy of creation. In our mind's eye, we visualize these seeds of peace and observe as they begin to appear in the palm of our hand. The intent and the intention are created.

We see the soil into which these seeds will be planted. We prepare the soil for these seeds. There may be weeds or obstacles that must be removed before we plant the seeds of peace. The weeds and obstacles represent the beliefs and myths that may consciously or unconsciously prevent the seeds from germinating.

We observe as the seeds of peace are planted. We visualize these seeds as they begin to germinate and sprout. We continue to tend and to nourish the soil in which the seeds have been planted. The weeds of doubt and uncertainty are removed. The soil is watered and provided with nutriments of faith and knowing. We watch the seedlings manifest into plants and trees that bear the fruits and flowers of peace—fruits and flowers that, as they mature, ripen and create new seeds, new manifestations of peace and life. Seeds and manifestations of peace that we can share with others.

The intent has manifested into the intention.

A Practice

A practice is a way of life, a way of being. Begin a daily practice. Create an intention for each day. Perhaps to trust that what Spirit provides to us each day is for the greatest evolution and growth of our soul.

Each morning, focus on the essence of this intention and then release the essence of this intention to Spirit. Allow the experience of the day to occur, without judgment or attachment. Let everything be as it is.

Each night, we allow ourselves to bring the experience of the day into the center of our awareness and our being. We observe. We receive the experience of the day in stillness, even if this stillness is the stillness between the breaths. We allow the integration of the day's journey into the soul of our being. We accept the experience as it is. No judgment. No attachment. We let go of that which no longer serves us, no longer feeds our soul. We then give thanks for the gift of life this day.

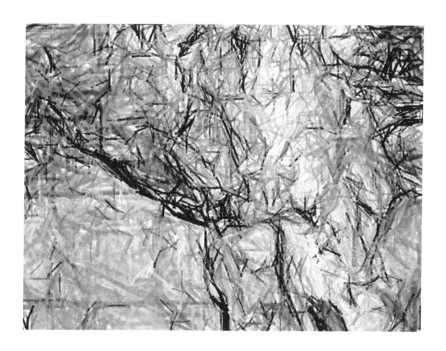

CHAPTER SEVENTEEN

PAIN, SUFFERING, AND VICTIMHOOD

The shaman works not only at the energetic, but also with the myths and stories we tell ourselves that may support the disease and turmoil in our life. Once traumatized we often tell and retell the stories of the trauma and wounding that we have suffered to all who will listen. While some may experience healing through the retelling of the story, many will re-traumatize themselves and those around them with each retelling.

Myths of Entitlement and Disempowerment

When we need something from someone else, or when we ask our gods to serve us if we worship them, then we create myths of entitlement and disempowerment. In entitlement and disempowerment, we create victimhood.

Pain happens. It is how we respond to the painful event that defines our growth. Divorce occurs. Job loss happens. Illness or cancer may devastate a physical body. The growth and healing come not from denying the events that have occurred or from spontaneous cure of a disease, but by how one lives life, how one grows and moves forward in the face of a perceived adversity. Is one paralyzed by the event? Does one wallow in the suffering assigned to this event by society, or does one use the event to begin one's healing journey?

Suffering is the story, the myth we decide to live when we choose to be a victim. We create a disempowering story or myth, which creates the beliefs of who we are or how we should be, which then creates our reality. A reality based on limiting and disempowering beliefs we hold as truth. A truth that may be based on the beliefs and experiences of others. Think of the small child who is running and falls. This child looks up to see the reaction of the parents before he knows whether to cry or laugh. The reaction of the parent may be based upon their truths and beliefs of a world that is safe or one that is predatory.

We create the story of victimhood. We become addicted to our story of suffering. The brain is unable to differentiate between the initial event and the subsequent retelling of the trauma. The retelling of the event is as real to the body as the first time the event occurred. Held in a state of heightened vigilance, our body responds physiologically to the perceived trauma.

This response includes the production of cortisol and adrenaline, the stress hormones activated in the fight-or-flight response to danger. This constant state of heightened vigilance and stress affects the brain and weakens the immune system. We become susceptible to illness and to turmoil. We become the victim.

Triangle of Disempowerment

The triangle of disempowerment is a triad of energy anchored by the archetypal roles of the victim, the perpetrator, and the rescuer.

This triangle of disempowerment is a system of energy not unlike an eddy in a stream. The energy within the eddy is caught, flowing around and around in a circle. Individuals held within the victim triangle are in the grip of this eddy. It is a vicious cycle that consumes energy without releasing anyone from the hold of this triangle. One is paralyzed in this eddy as the current of life flows past. It is full circle as we each shift our roles as victim, rescuer, or perpetrator, back and forth, going nowhere.

When we become the victim, we ask to be rescued. We are entitled to be rescued. Yet when we are addicted to victimhood, to suffering, we really do not wish to be rescued. In fact, we may respond with anger to another who offers to rescue us as they present their terms of the rescue. When we offer our help to someone who we perceive is asking to be rescued, we ask to be rewarded for our actions. This asking is of course unbeknownst to us, as we subconsciously demand obedience to the terms of our rescue. When the one we try to rescue refuses to do as we want them to do, that is, to reward us with the behavior or gratitude we desire of them, or when we fail to rescue them from their addiction to suffering, we become disempowered. We become angry. We think they are ingrates who are no longer worthy of our help. We are now the victim entitled to be rescued from our hurt and our anger. Yet we also become the perpetrator: "Do as I ask of you. Live my reality, and you will be rewarded. Don't do as I ask of you, and I will abandon you."

So as the victim, we call in the need to be rescued, often without really wanting to be rescued. The rescuer responds, offering his help. The victim continues as the victim, refusing the terms of help offered by the rescuer. The rescuer becomes angry, taking upon themselves the role of the victim, while the victim, who now sees the would-be rescuer as a perpetrator, strikes back as a perpetrator against the rescuer, or goes deeper into the victim role. The rescuer, now angered at the victim, then pushes back against the victim and indeed becomes a perpetrator.

Suffering

Humans are addicted to suffering and to living a victim lifestyle. We serve our gods and they serve us. We strive to be rescued. We demand to be rescued. *Look at me. Listen to my story. I am a victim of illness, of my ancestors, of life.* We create a myth of victimhood and entitlement that forms our beliefs and creates our reality, a reality of suffering and disempowerment.

Pain happens. Suffering, and living as the victim of circumstances, is a choice. Suffering or victimhood is not the painful trauma which caused or was associated with an event, but it is the myth we create around the trauma or the event. This myth creates the beliefs and reality of our existence, and the gods who we will serve.

Look at the stories we tell and retell to anyone who will listen. How do these stories serve us? How do they keep us safe? How do they keep us disempowered? How do they entitle us? How do they keep us in the triad of victim, rescuer, or perpetrator? Are these stories of wounding, stories of betrayal, stories of defectiveness, or are they stories of joy and beauty?

To heal, we must stop telling the story of the trauma. We open ourselves to change. No matter how unfortunate or devastating an experience seems to be, we allow ourselves to discover the lessons and opportunities that the universe has presented. We do not ignore the reality of the painful events that have occurred in life, but we choose instead not to suffer, not to retell or relive these traumatic events as the victim.

We reframe these events as part of our soul's journey through life and find the gifts and the opportunity for growth and healing that the experiences offer us. We honor those who we may perceive harmed us as our teachers, rather than as the agents of evil. We create a story of compassion and of empowerment rather than of victimhood. We create the journey of the hero. The journey that transforms us from the victim of our wounds and life's circumstances into one who is whole and in harmony with the all that is. This worldview empowers and releases us from being the wounded one, the victim pleading to be rescued. We take responsibility for our life and life choices. To this end, we might look at the journey and events occurring in our life as a representation of our soul's desire to learn and evolve in this realm of existence we describe as human.

When there is turmoil, illness, or emotional upset in our life, rather than blaming others, what if instead we were to look without judgment or ego as to how our behaviors and actions may have contributed to the current situation? When we become an observer of life, we are no longer a victim.

Victimhood feeds, and may be fed by, the core beliefs of wounding, betrayal, separation, defectiveness (worthlessness), abuse, or abandonment. When we transcend these beliefs and become the observer, we may create a world of health, a world of wholeness, and a world of beauty. When we release the role of victim, rescuer, or perpetrator, we no longer waste energy chasing the ghosts that consume our energy and paralyze our movement. We are no longer trapped in eddies of suffering and anger.

Healing occurs when we step out of the triangle of disempowerment and observe our actions and interactions with others. We become the observer, not the observed. We see who we are through the eyes of the observer, not through the eyes of the victim, or through the lens of fear and illness. We become an observer of life. One who has no attachment, no judgment, to the outcome of an event that has occurred, or to an event that might occur in the future. We are free to flow with the current of life.

When we change the myths that create our reality, then our world vision, beliefs, and reality change. Our gods change. We come into ayni—into right relationship and harmony—with these new gods and myths to create a world in which we may thrive. Supported by these new myths and beliefs of creation, our gods and our reality become one with Spirit.

To change our myths, we must first own and then honor the myths that we have been living. We give thanks and gratitude for who we have been, for the reality and the gods who we served and who served us, for it was our reality, our beliefs, and these gods that have brought us to where we are now.

Take a moment now and ask, "Who are the gods I serve? Who are the gods who serve me? What are the myths and demands of these gods?"

CHAPTER EIGHTEEN

PROJECTION, A PORTAL TO OUR SHADOW

When we become the observer, we are no longer a victim, a perpetrator, or a rescuer. We step away from the myths that have held that "*they* are the problem, not me." We begin to see what we could not see before, the beliefs, myths, and judgments that have created and held *them* as the problem. Yet sometimes we may be blindsided by something we cannot see. This something we cannot see is our shadow. That dark side of the moon the great mountains told me about after the journey to Apu Huaman Lipa in 2013.

To review, our projection is that hidden part of us that fears, in fact knows, we are unsafe because of *them*, that it is *they* who threaten the status quo, the very existence of our being. It is our projection that *they* are the cause of all that is wrong in life and that the world would be a better place without *them*. *They* make us full of anger, rage, guilt, and blame. We may never have met *them*. We may never have spoken to *them*. *Those people, those democrats, those republicans, those gays, those rednecks . . .*

But we know *they* are different and a threat to all that we believe and all that we allow to define us. *They* make us uncomfortable for *they* are the ones who threaten the unconscious myths and truths of our being. The truths that have guided us blindly as to what is right or wrong or who we can or should be.

On the journey to health, our projections become the mirrors that reflect our shadow. When we find ourselves blaming someone else for our feelings, actions, or beliefs, it is a good bet that we are projecting our shadow upon a group or individual. When we take ownership of our projections, we bring light and awareness to our shadows. Illumination of our shadow may be facilitated through identification of the belief we hold, ownership of this belief, transformation of this belief, and as we create a vision that energizes a new path and way of being.

Our Shadows and Projections

Our shadow and its projections influence the course of our journey and the destination at which we arrive. This influence may cloud our vision or provide us with false coordinates from which we orient and navigate our path to wholeness. The false coordinates and the underlying projection may lead us into a world that is unsafe. As we focus on this unsafe world, we may bring forth the manifestation of false demons that we must fight and annihilate if we are to live. Unconsciously, it may even be our true self we are denying and demonizing through the guise of others.

We may stop our projections and bring light to our shadow through the creation of a vision statement. A vision statement becomes an image that commands our subconscious to go in a new direction and on a new path. A vision statement guides our soul's journey. A vision statement is different than an affirmation, which consists only of words, the language of the mind. The vision statement speaks the language of the soul, the language of myths, imagery, and poetry.

When we create a vision statement for our journey, we reset our inner compass, we create new maps. We give ourselves permission to experience the mystery of life and explore the desires and dreams of our being. Through the process of creating and embodying a vision statement, we can clear the fog, recalibrate the coordinates, and true the course of our journey to wholeness and health.

To create a vision statement, we need first to identify the problem and the projection that have created a belief where we hold another responsible for our state of being. The belief might be: "You make me unhappy in this relationship" or "This situation makes me angry, upset, etc." The problem is "... unhappy in the relationship." "You make me ..." is the projection.

Once we have identified the problem and seen the projection, we must next own the projection. To take ownership of our projection and bring light to our shadow, we must acknowledge our participation and claim the belief that we are projecting. We claim ownership as we shift the wording of our belief from "You make me ..." into the first person. Now instead of "You make me unhappy," or "You make me angry," we stop the projection and reclaim our power. We now say, "When I am unhappy, I cannot be happy in any relationship," or "When I am angry, I cannot experience peace or joy."

Once we have taken ownership of our belief, we can change the belief. When we change our belief, we are no longer held hostage by the unconscious projections of our shadow. The vision statement speaks directly to our soul and radiates our intention to the universe. The statement might go something like this: "As I allow myself to experience joy and happiness, I bring joy and happiness into my relationship and to those who surround me." Or the vision statement of our journey may be "As I experience calmness, I experience peace and stillness within me and around me."

When we have taken ownership of our projections, our life changes; we are no longer at the mercy of unconscious forces shaping our beliefs. We may find resistance in this process as we hear our ego protest loudly again and again that "I am not the problem, *they* are." When this occurs just ask the ego to entertain the question as a hypothetical: "What if I was the problem—how would I own it?"

The next step in this process is to create an image that captures the experience and essence of our desired journey. An image that speaks to our soul. This might be the image of ourselves as we experience the playfulness of a happy puppy, or the awe and beauty of the setting sun. Perhaps it is the experience of acceptance and of belonging as we are held by Mother Earth, nourished by the warmth of her sun, or as we sit in the stillness of a mountain meadow. We must allow the experience and the image that has come to us to develop without interference of the mind.

We allow all the senses of our body, mind, and soul to participate and be informed through the experience of this moment. We then invite the essence of this image to infuse the cells, the molecules, and the atoms of our body. We sense the essences of peace, security, and joy that now nourish our physical body. We allow the essence of this image and the experience of this vision to inform our mind as our thoughts, beliefs, and maps harmonize with this new image of our life. We become aware of how our soul is fed through this image.

Finally, we wish to integrate the essence of this new energy into our body, mind, and spirit. There may be a song or a mythical character to whom we relate that allows us to incorporate this new us into the matrix of our energetic being. We may become aware of a new way we stand, speak, or move that reflects this new sense of empowerment and freedom.

The Projections We Create

The act of facing our own discomfort, and seeing through the darkness of our shadow, is a required step on the journey of awareness and healing. Remember that projection is a mirror through which we may see our shadow. Through ownership of our projection, we take the first step toward bringing our shadow into consciousness. When we see our shadow, we no longer need to project it upon another.

We understand that through our shadow's unconscious judgments, we are creating a deflection of that which we wish not to see or feel; that truth which we wish not to acknowledge as our own. The pain, the conflicted desires, the source of unhappiness or anxiety we carry within our shadow and project upon others. This is the truth and discontent of our soul we project upon another that we may not have to face it within ourselves. The self, we know, if revealed will be scorned by some and pitied by others.

Perhaps this is a good time to look at our shadow and the projections we create in our lives. From a place of compassion and honesty, let us create a list of those individuals or groups of people who we blame or hold responsible for the conditions of our life and the status of the world in which we live. Then without judgment or attachment to what has been, let us identify the problem, own the projection, and then create a vision statement to lead us forward into a new and empowering life.

As we explore the darkness of our shadow, we may encounter additional projections that prevent us from moving forward on our journey to health and harmony. Create a vision statement for each new projection that is encountered. These projections may also support beliefs that no longer serve the journey we are walking. Remember, in ceremony our energetic field may be cleansed and energetic blockages transformed. Bring these newly discovered beliefs into a sand painting or take them to a fire ceremony to be honored and released (see appendix). Repeat these rituals or ceremony whenever or wherever a blockage or doubt arises.

Create a New Myth

Now it is time to create the new myths that will support the new gods and the new beliefs that will create a new reality. A reality free from the myths and expectations of others, free of the unconscious projections of our shadow, and free of the archetypal energies of the victim triangle. These are the new myths of creation where we have found the light and the power within our own selves to manifest our dreams and desires. It is a time when we have transcended the old and integrated the new.

To create these new myths and this new reality, we will embark upon a journey of creation. We will engage and speak to our soul through image, story, and metaphor. Let us begin this journey now as we engage life as if it is a fairy tale. The journey into a new reality might begin with *"Once upon a time there was a myth maker weaving a tale of empowerment and creativity, a tale of..."* We might use images such as the images found on the major arcana of the tarot cards to fuel our creative process. These images tap into the archetypal themes of human existence. Or perhaps we might use pictures found in a magazine that resonate with the desires of our soul. As we view these images of life, it is the essence of creation to which our soul has connected, not the literal image depicted in the pictures that we have engaged. Some might call this a vision board for the soul.

As these myths are written and a new reality created, we will begin to experience a world of joy and beauty. It will be a world that encompasses compassion and courage; a world that will allow for compromise and forgiveness. In this world we will experience the gifts of bounty and of abundance.

We, as the weaver of these myths, will create a reality in which there is no longer a victim, rescuer, or perpetrator; a reality where there is no longer an addiction to suffering. We will create a world where our thoughts and actions will be guided by light and through love to bring forth peace and tranquility. In this world we will experience wholeness and health.

The path to wholeness is what mythology calls the Hero's Journey. The story of the wounded healer who rises above the turmoil of adversity to live in peace and harmony with all that is.

The wounded healer is the self that creates a reality of awareness and of conscious living. This is a reality free of our shadow and the roles we have been assigned. A reality where there is no longer a *"them"* who defines us; there is only the I, walking the path of wholeness and health.

The self that walks this journey transcends that which no longer serves the journey. This self creates a reality free of the beliefs and judgments of others. This is a reality created by us, the observer, freed from the confines of the victim triangle and the outlived myths of creation.

We As Creator

When we step into awareness and choice, we become the weaver of our myths and the creator of our life. We create a reality that reflects who we are, who we can be. We choose what roles or myths we wish to accept and those we wish to discard. We as creator transform and define these roles. Remember, the roles we create will no longer carry the beliefs, judgments, or expectations of others.

In fact, the roles no longer carry the beliefs that we have held as truths all these years. We create the roles and beliefs that serve us now. We can write the myth and the reality in which culture and society honor the roles we have created. We can write the story of the mother who not only serves her children but serves herself as well.

Own the New Myth

Once this new myth has been spun, we wish to weave its essence and the power of the myth's creative potential into the tapestry of our being. This weaving and the assimilation of the myth into our myth of creation bring forth new possibilities and the potential for the manifestation of a new reality.

We created and told this tale in the third person. To own this myth, to embody its essence into the tapestry of our life and our being, we must take ownership of our creation. Let us tell this story, this myth of creation, from the first person, as the "I." *"I am the myth maker, weaving a tale of empowerment and creativity. A tale of joy, beauty, harmony, health, and wholeness . . ."*

Reading the fairy tale in first person allows us to own the myth, to embody the myth and to bring life to the soul of the myth. As we take ownership of our myth, as we embody its essence into the tapestry of our being, we transform what was once outside of us and separate to within. When we have taken ownership, we may begin to grow the seeds of possibility and experience this new reality as part of who we are. We may engage this new myth with our senses as we taste joy, as we smell beauty, or as we hear

205

the voices of the myth maker within us. We may feel wholeness and abundance within our being and experience the sense of health once again.

Go ahead, announce this myth to the gods and goddesses of the cosmos, *"Once upon a time that is now, I became the myth maker of my life. I created a life in which I experience joy, I experience health, I experience love and light, a life in which I experience..."*

When the myths of life and of creation feed our soul, our soul and our being are in harmony. Our voice is strong. We resonate with life. We are in ayni.

Now from a place of stillness and peace, and as the observer of our own body and soul, let us experience and then ask, "How does this myth live within and around me?" We may take note of how or if we have changed as we ask: "Do I stand differently? Do I move differently? Do I speak differently? Am I breathing differently? Does the air I breathe feel different, taste different, perhaps softer, gentler, or sweeter?

"Through which filters am I now engaging life? Are the flowers that nourish my soul more colorful, more fragrant? Is my soul responding to a new song, a new rhythm or beat?"

Now let us allow ourselves to observe without judgment or attachment where or how the myth may feel or be incomplete within our being. Ask of the self: "Is my voice weak? Is there stuttering or hesitancy as I tell the myth? Is there a sense of uneasiness or heaviness experienced in the body? Do words feel stuck? Are there emotions such as fear or doubt that arise, activating the fight, flight, or freeze response within me?" These may be clues that we need to go deeper into our awareness and healing to find additional complexes of subconscious beliefs and blockages that might derail our journey.

If the myth is not fully alive, we may call upon the spirits of the wind or of fire to help clear these blockages. Just as the wind might dissipate a dark cloud that covers the peaks of a mountain, we may call upon our breath to blow through and release the limiting beliefs held within our being. Perhaps we might ask our breath to act as a billow to bring fire, passion, and life to the embers of these myths and in doing so consume that which no longer serves us.

Alternatively, we might place a stone over the area of our body where we sense the heaviness, then direct our breath to move the heaviness or blockage into the body of the stone. Lastly, we may choose to take the issues that have arisen to ceremony to be transformed through the power of fire or of a mandala created on the earth.

Visualization

Visualization guides the journey of the soul. When we have fully connected with this new myth, we may visualize ourselves living this reality now. We may visualize the healed self. The self in which our body, mind, and soul are in health and wholeness.

Through visualization we may plant and feed the seeds of our journey. We may tend the soil or remove the weeds and obstacles that may entangle our journey. We may visualize the creation of new behaviors and the shedding of what has been. We may envision new pathways through which the neurons of our body will fire and respond to direct the journey of our soul. Pathways that are in balance, healthy, and supportive of our new myths and ways.

As we walk the path of the hero, we walk in peace, in wholeness, and in harmony. As we walk this journey, we will encounter the canyons of life. It is into these canyons that we will loudly shout our new myths of creation. We will then let the echoes of the canyons and voices of our myths resound as they become the whispers that reverberate through the cosmos and guide us through life.

CHAPTER NINETEEN

INVITE THE GODS TO LIVE WITH US

We have shed our roles. We have released the thoughts, the limiting beliefs, and the judgments that no longer serve who we are, or who we may become. We have created new myths that have brought forth new thoughts and new beliefs. We have owned and embodied these new myths and beliefs. We have consecrated new gods.

We know we have choice. We have free will to heal ourselves. We can choose to stay in an old familiar reality, or we can choose to embrace the myths and the gods of a new reality. Healing occurs when we choose to embody the healed, to embrace the new myths, and to live with the new gods. Let us invite the gods of health, wholeness, joy, love, and beauty to come and live with us.

How will we nourish these gods? How will we worship them? What gifts do we bring to them? What beliefs, what reality, what myths must we sacrifice to appease them so they will support us on the journey of wholeness and of health? What are the new myths, the new beliefs that are required to support these gods and the new reality they have brought forth? How must we honor the gods we once worshiped, that once served us, that they may be fully released and allowed to rest? These are the questions we must ask and be willing to answer when we invite the gods to live with us.

A Final Note

Throughout this book I have mentioned free will and choice as if one could wake up one morning, flip a switch, and change lifelong patterns of belief and behavior. For a lucky few this might be the case. For the rest of us, however, we may find the pursuit of free will and choice is a lifelong journey of discovery. A journey that brings awareness to, and understanding of, the unconscious myths and patterns that have created our life. It is through the choice we make each day to understand, to dig deeper into our shadow and the realm of the unconscious, that we may allow our authentic self to be revealed.

PART FOUR

OF INTEGRATION AND UNDERSTANDING

THE JOURNEY CONTINUES

March 2012, Madre de Dios

I stood at the edge of the darkness, illuminated by a scant flicker of light offered by a torch that was a hundred yards behind me. I had stood at this same spot many nights this past week, facing that invisible barrier of darkness, frozen, unable to take the step into the unknown.

Fear rose within me as I anticipated taking the step. It was a step that would take me into my shadow, a step that would illuminate the darkness of being and allow me to experience the light of creation. It was a step immersed in trust. Trust that the universe was supportive and benign. Trust that I would be held, that I would be embraced by the darkness of the jungle, supported and nourished by the unknown energies of life.

I thought of what Alan had said just a few weeks before: "As we approach the contact boundary, we must breathe. We must use our breath to carry us through the moment of anticipation, the moment of fear, through those invisible barriers that stop us from moving forward on our journey of life."

As I took the first step into the darkness of the jungle, fear began to rise within me. The darkness devoured all visible light as the entanglements of the vines and the voices of the jungle consumed me. Frozen in the fear of my expectations, paralyzed, unable to be in the moment, I stopped breathing. There was no life force, only the stagnation of death. Then I remembered Alan's words and I breathed. The breath carried me through the death I was experiencing, through the blockage, through the fear and into the experience of life once again.

It is in that moment in which we succumb to the fear, in which we stop breathing, that fear overtakes us. It is in that moment when we stop engaging the known or the unknown due to our fears that we begin to die as we retreat from life.

CHAPTER ONE

A RETURN TO THE GARDENS OF ESALEN

A month earlier I had returned to the gardens and springs of Esalen. I would be participating in a weeklong workshop focused on Gestalt therapy. I had chosen the workshop—or perhaps I should say the universe had chosen the workshop for me—as I browsed through the winter catalogue.

Throughout life I have avoided conflict. I have run from conflict. I have been a chameleon to avoid conflict. Now I have conflict thrust upon me. Conflict began the first night of the workshop. When asked, "Why?" I answered in truth: I did not know why.

I honestly did not know why I was in this workshop. I had trusted the tracking of my pendulum, as I browsed through the winter catalogue, to choose a workshop for me to attend. This explanation did not sit well with the group of twelve individuals who had come to study with Alan Schwartz. Alan was an early pioneer in both Gestalt therapy and Humanistic Psychology. He was an esteemed member of the Esalen faculty, a guru of sorts. These were his groupies who I had encountered.

This week, the way I spoke, the way I walked, my beliefs and approaches to life were challenged and questioned by those in the room. It seemed if I opened my mouth or sat in the same or different space each day, I created conflict. When I spoke of my plans to be in the Amazon that month, my intentions were challenged. Yet each day, each session, I returned to face this conflict.

We are informed that life is an experiment. That everything we do in life is an experiment, a hypothesis of the moment, a moment in which we measure the experience of our past with the expectation of our future. We learn experiments cannot be wrong; they just are. We may add our own personal attachments to an experiment, but the experiment without attachment is just an experiment. It is only the question we have posed: "I wonder what will happen if . . .?" There is no success or failure. If it works, great, if not, great. There is no investment in the outcome as it is just an experiment.

One morning we participated in an experiment to assess the power and force of the spoken word upon individuals. The class was split in half between the women and men. The men stood on one side of the room, their backs toward the women, who stood against the opposite wall. The men were asked just to be present, to note their experience, while the women were asked to connect with any emotions of anger, rage, or hatred they may hold toward the men in their life. Next, they were asked to direct and vocally release the words attached to these emotions upon us, the men in the class.

As we were being verbally assaulted with their words of anger and hatred, we physically experienced the force and power of the emotions that were attached to these words. We felt the guilt, the shame, and the anger that these women had experienced from men throughout their lives. I, as many of the men also experienced, felt pummeled and exhausted upon completion of this five-minute experiment. The women conversely felt lightness and release as a result of this experiment.

Fields of Energy and the Contact Boundary

Later we learned about fields of energy that may affect and organize our journey through life. There are fields we call organic. These are the fields of energy generated by our physical body. There are fields that are non-organic. For this week, we are told this field of the non-organic is comprised of the students in the class.

There is the field of the foreground generated by the environment we inhabit at this moment. Lastly there is the field of the background comprised of everything we have learned and experienced in life. These fields are multilayered, always present. These fields influence us with every breath of life.

During this week, I would learn of and experience the contact boundary. The contact boundary is an invisible barrier that stops us from obtaining our full potential in life. It is where our mind, soul, and body begin to engage a perceived threat. A threat perhaps unknown to our conscious mind yet recognized and carried by our fields of energy. It is the point in space and time where fear may overwhelm our rational mind and the instinct of survival overtakes our being.

We are asked, "What is it that keeps us from being present, that does not go away, or that we must overcome to be fully available to experience the here and the now?" We are told this recurring force that prevents us from being present is our gestalt. The gestalt is an organized structure or pattern of energy we repeatedly carry into the moment that stops us, that prevents us from being present. The moment is defined as a twelve-second cycle of time. We are told every twelve seconds this cycle of time, our state of being present, resets itself.

In the moment of encounter with our gestalt, we may experience something outside of our comfort zone, something we must face, that we must deal with or walk away from. Consciously or unconsciously we know something has disturbed us, that disharmony has been created in the homeostasis of our organic field. We may become paralyzed, reactionary, or we may even begin to flee. In these actions of avoidance, we begin to die to new experiences. We begin to die to life.

The point in time and space where this moment of encounter occurs is the contact boundary. We are asked to look at our behavior at the contact boundary. Do we reveal ourselves or conceal ourselves? When we reveal ourselves, we show up. We claim our voice and the right for our voice to be heard. We affirm our existence and our right to manifest our own destiny. When we conceal ourselves, we shrink away. We give away our existence, our voice, and our right to manifest our individual destiny to an invisible force that stops us from being present.

When we conceal ourselves, we give our power to the myths and beliefs of others, and to the voices they have brought forth within us. The voices of fear, the voices that say it is too hard, that it cannot be different. The same voices that say *I am not good enough*, or *I don't deserve better.*

We learn that how we react in any situation may be dependent upon three factors, three questions we ask consciously or unconsciously of ourselves at that moment in time and space. The first questions deal with inclusion: "Do I belong here?" "Do I have the right to exist?"

The next questions invoke authority: "How and why do I belong here? How do I stack up with the others? How do I relate to the others?" And finally, "How am I in balance here?" We each carry the masculine and feminine within our being—how does this situation resonate with what our balance is at this moment? We might ask, "Are we here to gestate, to create, or to receive?"

We hold our breath at times of risk, and in the face of fear. Alan tells us to use our breath, to breathe through the fear, to breathe through the moment of risk to reveal ourselves. In revealing ourselves, we begin to deconstruct that which stands in our way to experience the now moment. We claim our right to exist, to be heard, and to control our own destiny.

During this week with each boundary we face, we breathe. At least for twelve seconds we breathe, that we may be present and experience the moment. Then we are free to move forward, to move on to our next contact boundary, to experience the next gestalt on our journey through life.

Upon conclusion of the workshop, we sat together and expressed our thoughts about one another. It was universal. They all informed me that I had not experienced or understood gestalt. Then, Alan spoke, and his words were life-giving. "I had my doubts, not sure why Jim was in this workshop, yet he has been present. Throughout this week he was present as he faced his contact boundary. This workshop has been his gestalt through which he breathed."

The experience of the workshop was the heart of conflict, and I, with each breath, breathed through the contact boundary to reveal myself.

The Generic Rights

Alan spoke of the five generic rights to which each human is entitled. These rights include the right to exist, the right to stand, the right to be a person, the right to control one's own destiny in life, and the right to love and be loved. It was not until the following month on my journey into the Amazon that I realized the significance of these rights and of the workshop I had just attended.

Alan and his wife were quite concerned about my safety as I began that journey to the Amazon. I will share an email to Alan Schwartz written after my return from the jungle that speaks to the power of these rights.

April 2011, email to Alan Schwartz:

> Alan,
>
> I have returned from the Amazon quite alive and well. During the week, I experienced the death of who I am, who I was, and who I will become. I relived the trauma, the events, and the karma of these lives as my body and my soul were torn apart, dismembered, and as I died to who I was (at least up to twelve seconds ago). Only now do I begin to understand the synchronicity in play, and the reason for showing up and meeting you and the others in the workshop last month at Esalen.

The constant of my journey in the jungle was both "the here and the now" as well as "the contact boundary." Forget about experiencing any fear as I approached the contact boundary. I was immediately thrown into the extreme of the event, into the depth of the fear, or of the emotion that needed to be healed and released.

There was no concealment from myself, only revelation. Surviving the experience only by breathing through it and bringing myself back to the present moment, to "the here and the now." Often, there was not a body to return to in the present, only the moment.

The purpose of the work with the jungle shamans became quite clear. The work was to deconstruct the armor, the blockages which no longer served me. Another purpose was to create new supports which would allow me to embody the five generic rights: the right to exist, the right to stand, the right to be a person, the right to control my destiny, and the right to love and be loved. I will add a sixth, the right to have a voice and for my voice to be heard.

The right to exist and the right to stand became the portals and the anchors that allowed me to reenter this plane of existence and consciousness, on more than one occasion, during the work. It was only as I fully let go, and healed at all levels of my body, mind, and soul, that my energy field would clear, and embodiment of the right would occur. This might mean re-experiencing or giving voice to the trauma or event.

There was a need to bring compassion and to honor the wounding. Fully letting go of the judgment, the reaction, or the belief that no longer served me, only then did I, could I, embody the right. As I embodied these rights, I began to realize my own power to create my reality and my stories, to become the author of my life.

The importance of rest and nourishment during this process of embodiment is well recognized by you. At Esalen, the elements of nature and our connection to Mother Earth offered us a place for deep rest and integration of the healing. We were nourished by the sacred waters and the bounty of the gardens. Our star brothers and sisters welcomed us as they shared their wisdom. The voices of the ocean spoke, as the waves crashed silently beneath the cliffs of our unconscious, to bring forth new songs of life.

So, too, in the Amazon did I experience this deep healing as I was cleansed by the waters of the Madre de Dios river, nourished by the fertile soils of the earth, and revitalized by the life force of the jungle. Here in nature the plants spoke their wisdom and brought forth healing as they shared their medicine. The process of embodiment and crystallization occurred.

In these settings of beauty and safety, the body receives the energy and then informs the mind and soul facilitating the healing process. Yet healing facilitated by the shaman is also occurring at the level of the energetic and the soul. It is in the changing of the energy field and in creation of new mythic maps, new stories, that healing occurs at the level of the soul that then informs the mind and the body.

Alan, I reiterate the statement I made to you one night. You are a gifted shaman. You read the energy of the individuals and the group, then transformed this energy, created new maps, and assisted and empowered each of us to use this energy for our healing.

Who knew Gestalt therapy was an ancient shamanic practice?

With gratitude . . .

Review of the Generic Rights

We have the right to exist, for our soul to be present, to manifest in an energetic matrix that is of human form. To occupy space. To be.

We have the right to stand. To occupy the space that we choose. To connect with the foundation of Earth. To have the vision to see our path from the vista above the canopy of the jungle.

We have the right to be human, and in such, to treat and to be treated with love and compassion, to experience joy and beauty. As humans it is our obligation to treat all forms of consciousness—be it animal, plant, or rock—with dignity, respect, and compassion.

We have the right to love and be loved. This is not just romantic love, but the love of compassion. The love of the soul for the colors of the setting sun, the fragrance of the flowers, be they roses, gardenias, or night-blooming jasmine. It is the love of the cactus flowers blooming in the early hours of the morning for the life-giving rains.

We have the right to have a voice, and for our voice to be heard. This is the voice of our truths, our reality. With this voice we become self-referencing.

We have the right to control our own destiny. We have the right to choose and bring forth the manifestation of our dreams and beliefs. Beliefs that some may say are impossible, destinies others may say are improbable.

When...

When we invoke our authority, when we claim and embody the generic rights, we reveal our self. We step from the myths, the judgments of others. We step from the victim triangle, and we become both an observer and creator of life. We begin to understand the mystery of who we are becoming and the path we have walked. We see our worthiness. We remember who we are and who we are becoming. We once again see the journey of our soul. We are present, here and now, for life and all of its mysteries.

Claim and Experience These Rights Now

Let us take this moment in time to claim and invoke ownership of these rights as we, in the first person, announce our authority to the universe:

I have the right to exist, for my soul to be present to manifest in an energetic matrix which is of human form. To occupy space. To be.

I have the right to stand. To occupy the space that I choose. To connect with the foundation of Earth. To have the vision to see my path from the vista above the canopy of the jungle.

222

I have the right to be human and as such to treat and to be treated with love and compassion, to experience joy and beauty. As a human being it is my obligation to treat all forms of consciousness—be it animal, plant, or rock—with dignity, respect, and compassion.

I have the right to love and be loved. This is not just romantic love, but the love of compassion. The love of the soul for the colors of the setting sun, the fragrance of the flowers, be they roses, gardenias, or night-blooming jasmine. It is the love of the cactus flowers blooming in the early hours of the morning for the life-giving rains.

I have the right to have a voice and for my voice to be heard. This is the voice of my truths, my reality. With this voice I become self-referencing.

I have the right to control my own destiny. I have the right to choose and bring forth the manifestation of my dreams and beliefs. Beliefs that some may say are impossible, destinies others may say are improbable.

When...

When I invoke my authority, when I claim and embody the generic rights, I reveal myself. I step from the myths, the judgments of others. I step from the victim triangle and become both an observer and creator of life. I begin to understand the mystery of who I am becoming and the path I have walked. I see my worthiness; I remember who I am and who I am becoming. I see the journey of my soul. I am present here and now for life and all of its mysteries.

CHAPTER TWO

CASA DE DOM IGNACIO

"If you are expecting to arrive at the Casa and have God descend in front of you and say, 'You are now healed, my child, you may go home,' you are probably going to be disappointed."

The Casa Guide, 2011

The Casa, 2012

My wife and I came to Brazil without expectation, and without need or desire for healing. We came instead with curiosity about a man known as João de Deus, John of God. We came to Brazil to experience João and the Casa de Dom Ignacio. We were not disappointed.

Established in 1979, the Casa is located near the small rural town of Abadiânia, about an hour's drive south of the capital of Brazil. The Casa is described as a temple and spiritual hospital where individuals may receive physical, emotional, and spiritual healing. Open to all who seek healing, the experience is based upon the spiritualist doctrine, a commonly held belief in Brazil and South American countries.

The spiritualist doctrine embodies the belief that souls or spirits who are no longer incarnated in a human body continue to exist outside the human form and that these spirits may communicate with incarnate beings through individuals known as mediums. A medium serves as a channel for this communication.

There are mediums who maintain control and awareness of their bodies and thoughts as they channel the communications of a spirit, and there are mediums who fully incorporate the spirit, who fully give their corporal being over to the spirit. We are told John of God is such a medium. He is a full-trance medium, one who fully incorporates the spirit within his body.

Spiritualism puts forth that these spirits, these disincarnate beings, continue to serve humanity in much the same way as when incorporated in human form. Hence, there are those who may create chaos as they did in life, and there are those who are here to serve and bring healing and balance to individuals and the world. John of God is of service to this latter group of spirits as he offers his body to healers such as St. Ignatius of Loyola, King Solomon, Francisco Xavier, Dr. Augusto de Almeida, Dr. Jose Valdivino, and Dr. Oswaldo Cruz. It is the spirits of these individuals, these healers, that come forth thorough the corporal existence of João to create the elements necessary for healing.

My Intent

I wrote of my intent for the two weeks we are to be here at the Casa and with John of God. I wrote that the entities invited me to the Casa. That I am here to cleanse and to strengthen my body, my vessel, so that it will hold and attune to the highest frequency of divine energy. That this energy of the divine may flow from Spirit through me to assist others in their journey of healing. We went to the translator, who shortened my intent to two words, "spiritual development."

At the Casa we experience deep cleansing, balance, and attunement of our chakras as we bask in the pure energy of the crystalline baths. We are cleansed by the waters of the Cachoeira, the sacred waterfall. Our healing is supported by the water and the soups they give us daily that have been blessed by the spiritual entities of the Casa. Brought each day to our room, they nourish us as we convalesce from the spiritual surgeries we have undergone.

We connect in harmony with the energies of the Casa and with the spirits that support the Casa. We connect directly with the healing lands of the Casa and the surrounding fields. We sit for hours in meditation as we support the cleansing and healing processes of João and the embodied spirits. During the times of meditation and through the night, there are visitations by the healers of the Casa. There are downloads of wisdom and understanding, followed by deep rest and integration of what we have received.

Spiritual Surgery

It is announced that all who are here this afternoon will receive an intervention, will receive spiritual surgery. We have no need. We have not planned, have not desired, to participate in the surgery. This is an honor, a chance of a lifetime for most. We are skeptical. There is no opportunity to say, "No thank you, not what I need," as we begin to walk with scores of others through the two current rooms.

The first room is a room of cleansing. It is a room supported by the entities and the participants who have offered to assist in the cleansing of the energetic field of those who are about to be scanned by the entity embodied within João. In the second room are those from whom the energetic matrix of João can draw sustenance to support the embodied spirit within João.

We present ourselves to the entity embodied in João. Our field is scanned, perhaps touched by an outreached hand, and then we are given a script for passiflora, an herb that will carry the subtle essence of energy to support our individual healing. Then the entity incorporated with João waves us into a third room.

In this third room, we sit on benches. It seems only a few moments that we remain seated, but it is closer to forty minutes. There is an individual, a medium of the Casa, channeling and offering prayers in Portuguese for our journey of healing. Then a voice comes forth from the body of João: "You have received your operation. You are healed." We are told to rest for the next twenty-four hours, that our meals, our soup, will be brought to our rooms. "Now go. Rest."

By the time we pick up our herbs and get the taxi back to our *posada*, I am exhausted. I lie down and fall asleep. Several hours later, I am awakened by pain, as if a chisel is being hammered against the bones of my left ankle. The ankle that I severely sprained earlier that summer, in fact, most likely broke. The hammering and chiseling on my ankle continue for at least an hour. Then the discomfort ceases as quickly as it began. It has been almost six years since that night, and there has been no pain, no discomfort. There are visitations by spirit and deep sleep over the next twenty-four hours.

Writings

During our stay, I am guided through automatic writings and channeled downloads in which there are echoes of the wisdom and words of past teachers and of the journeys with the spirits of the plants. My understanding of the generic rights and of existence deepens. Below is a sample of the wisdom channeled and revealed as I sat overlooking the expanse of the valley in front of me.

- When we deny our truths, we deny our existence. Our truths stem from the agreements our soul made before we entered this realm.
- In healing, in fact in all of life's events, wherever we are is perfect. For this is exactly where the soul is to be at that moment, to grow and to evolve. Were an individual not in that state, at that given moment, the soul could not learn and evolve. When the soul does not learn its lesson, then it must continue to recreate events that will again give it an opportunity to learn and evolve. Perhaps health is a misnomer. Health may be a stagnant state or state of rest during which the lessons learned in disease are woven into the fabric of the soul.
- When we deny who we are, we deny the existence of our self. When we deny that we are Spirit, we deny the existence of Spirit.
- From where I stand in the universe, it does not matter where, I create the whole of what is around me. From each point the whole can be created, the holographic concept of creation.
- When it is said in the Bible "to stand or step before God," perhaps it is not the literal meaning to stand in front of God, but instead to step before the creation of God, into the creative template of God.
- The creative is the template of the creator. The creator does not exist prior to the creative. This is the concept of the etheric body being the template for the physical body, in that the physical body does not exist without the etheric template.
- This creative force or template may be what is referred to as the mother of God.
- The purple nebula is the god, the force, the creative force that is required for the creator to exist.
- The human race is attempting to separate and distance itself from nature and Spirit.

- If we are not one with the creative force, then we are sep-arate from it and do not exist within it. Then we do not exist as part of the whole. We, as human beings, will no longer exist in the world of Spirit or nature.
- When one denies the existence of what one knows as truth, one is out of harmony and in a state of disease. This is where illness and turmoil occur.
- I am a healer.
  I am a spiritual healer.
  I am a god.
  I am Spirit, I am creator, I am the creatrix, and I am the creative force.
  I am.
- What is it like to be "am"? "Am" feels dynamic, transform-ative, an active process. We are present as the "am." It is a state in which one has the right to call forth and manifest the right to exist. To control one's own destiny.
- In the "am" we are in the here and the now. We have the right to stand. To be an individual, to exist and stand alone as an individual part of the whole, not separate from the whole.
- What is it like to "be?" "Be" is passive, meditative, one with self, the purple nebula, one with all. The intent is not the "I wish to be" mentality, for that implies separation. The in-tent is just "be." Then I am not in the process of transforming, but in the state of "being." In this state, I am the mountain, I am the rock, and I am the river, for I am the creative force. We are one with Creator, one with the crea-tive force. We are the creative force. We have the right to exist, because we exist. Human beings can shape-shift from the state of "be" and become the "I am."
- The concept of "it is as it is." It (the situation or event) ex-ists without judgment as to what it is. There is acceptance of what is. There is no need for change. If one is always looking for what one does not have, then one will miss what one actually has.

- I have the right to have a voice and to speak my truth. To have and to hold my beliefs. To hold my beliefs as truth. To be in harmony, to be in balance, in ayni with my truth. When we are not in balance with our truth, we may become ill.
- The work we do as healers is for the growth and evolution of the soul. From within this plane of reality, we may not see the greater picture or the whole. The event that we or the client is experiencing may be for the greater good of the soul. And therefore, healing that we judge is necessary for another (or what we mistakenly think of as a cure) might not be for the greatest good of the soul.
- Healing. As a healer, we wish to attune lower energies to a higher level, not banish them. We transform them as we attune our client and the lower energies to the vibration of Spirit.
- In healing we:
  Access sacred space.
  Set intent.
  Attune to the rites of the creator, to become one with all.
  Attune with Spirit (Taitanchi).
  Attune with client.
  Allow the healing energies to be as one.
- For the healer, it is not about being a conduit or vessel for the energy. It is about being one with the energy. It is about being the energy.
- If we are a conduit or vessel, there is still friction. We are still separate from the energy. As healers, we become the energy. We are the light, the divine energy. We "are."
- To be a person. What is a person? We define a person as an individual who is part of the whole yet can be recognized as an individual. What creates the right to be a person? The ability to stand and be recognized within the whole for who we are as individuals. To hold our own consciousness, yet still be part of the whole.

- The ability to hold one's own truth is the right to be a person. Who am I? What is my truth? How does one know when one has found one's truth?
- Are there truths that are universally accepted? Are truths able to change over time?
- What is the right to be human? What does it mean to be human? What creates humanity? What defines us as humans? Selflessness, love, spirit, soul (individual vs. communal), to think—these abilities are all shared by other forms of life, animals, plants, etc.
- As humans we have the right to control our own destiny. We have the right to separate from nature, or so we choose to believe. For when we deny our truth, we deny our existence.
- As we connect to our spiritual guides and power animals, we are connecting with Spirit. They are a manifestation of Spirit and of divine energy. They are intermediaries between Spirit and individuals that function much like a transformer that converts electrical energy from 220 volts to 110 volts. The current, which is coming from Spirit, is reduced so that our field (human energy field) may access and utilize it. The current is reduced so that we may utilize it and not allow the current to fry our energy field. This is not to say that there are not individuals who can and do access the energy of Spirit directly.
- Walk in peace and grace. Do not search for the sacred but bring the sacred with every step and every breath.

A Sharing

Over the course of our stay, the entities come and go. They share their thoughts and their wisdom. They tell me they are here as consultants and as teachers for my clients, and for me. They will be present when called. Not just the entities of the Casa, but the healers of all lineages will be available to be summoned. I do not need to incorporate them as is done by John of God. I need only to hold space, and they will be present.

I am introduced to Doctor De Leon of Italy, a healer of the fifteenth century who is there to support this journey I walk. I have not asked, but I am told by the Casa entities that the deterioration of the brain will not get better, but it will not get worse either. That through this perceived misfortune, I have been opened to gifts. Gifts that had been blocked from my consciousness.

In the work with John of God, I realize it is not about being in the presence of John of God, that he is not the healer. João is the vessel to hold the healers. He becomes the energy of these healers, the energy of wholeness and health. Through our connection with Spirit, with Creator, we, too, may become this power, this force of creation.

I recall the intent I had written for our journey at the Casa, "That the energy of the divine may flow from Spirit through me." Perhaps now I would write, "To remember that I, that we are the energy and manifestation of the divine and of the Creator. That we are Spirit."

Chapter Three

The Wisdom Teachings

Let us remember the fundamental principle of life in the Andes is ayni. Ayni is that place of balance, of being in right relationship with all that is. When we are in balance, we are in harmony with the universe. When we are at peace with all that exists, then all in life is perfect just as it is. There is no illness, turmoil, or disease; there is no victim, rescuer, or doer. There is only life. There is only Spirit experiencing another face of Spirit. The sages of old understood these fundamental principles and lived in harmony with all of creation.

The sages were the medicine men and women who lived both within and outside of time. They were the holders of the ancient knowledge and knew the mysteries of creation. This body of knowledge and the mysteries of creation were collectively known as the "Wisdom Teachings." For these men and women, the teachings of these ways and the holding of this wisdom were not just an intellectual pursuit or a way of life—it *was* life. The sages knew the embodiment of this knowledge and the holding of this wisdom allowed them to become dreamers, myth weavers, and creators of life itself. According to legend and lore, the sages freely shared the gifts of these teachings with all who were ready.

During my training with Alberto and the indigenous healers of the Americas, the wisdom teachings of these great sages were shared with me. These same teachings are shared here today for others. With awareness and as we make a practice of these teachings, we, too, may embody their gifts. Gifts that will allow us to create a life of joy, beauty, and compassion; a life that is sourced from love and light.

Pain Happens

The sages tell us that pain happens in life, but that suffering is optional. Suffering is the story of victimhood we create around a traumatic event and continue to tell long after the actual event is over.

Each time we retell a story of suffering, whether to ourselves or to others, we may be retraumatized by the event. Let us remember in the primitive levels of the human brain, the brain is unable to differentiate the reliving of an unhealed traumatic event through story from the actual event. In the moment that we recall the story, the brain interprets our recalled story as happening in the present, not five years ago. We once again become a victim of the wounding.

The unhealed wound, now retriggered, activates the survival instincts. The adrenal glands respond with a massive release of adrenaline and cortisol that course through the blood vessels to infuse every cell of our body. Physiologically, our body, now prepared for an attack, is frozen in a state of hypervigilance, ready to flee or fight the ghosts of the past.

When the survival instincts are constantly and repeatedly activated, a physical and emotional toll is taken upon our bodies. We become fatigued, depressed, and ill. We become trapped and paralyzed in fear, unable to heal. We become a victim to our own story, our own creation. To heal we must stop the story of suffering.

Our Stories of Suffering

In Western society, we are addicted to our stories of suffering and to victimhood. We write, rewrite, and retell these stories of suffering to all who will listen. These may be stories of betrayal, deception, or the abuse by which we have been victimized. This addiction to suffering is embedded in the mythology of many cultures and religions. Who has not suffered hardship and toil as they were expelled from the gardens of their personal Eden?

The sages tell us we must take time to honor the pain we have experienced, but only when we have chosen to release the suffering embedded within our stories may we heal. They know only then will we be freed from the myths of our Eden.

Our Attachment

We are attached to our beliefs and our stories for they support the judgment we hold of ourselves. The judgment of worthlessness, defectiveness, and separation—these are just a few of the ways we attach ourselves to our beliefs, to our reality that we are the victim. The sages say that we must release our judgment and our attachment to what has been or what might be. Once we have released our attachments to what has been, we may create a new story. A story in which we are empowered and perfectly present in the current moment.

The sages speak of walking in beauty. With each step, each breath they take, they experience this beauty and are nourished by its essence. The sages see each moment as an opportunity to celebrate, partake, and live in the beauty of life. They know that all is perfect just as it is. What appears as an obstacle in life to some is seen by these men and women as an opportunity for growth and evolution.

The sages tell us to walk in fearlessness. The sages know when we walk in fearlessness, there is nothing to weaken us. There is nothing to engage. There is nothing that must be changed, nothing that needs to be changed. There is nothing to do. This is the place of non-doing.

In this place of non-doing, we flow with the current of the universe. We flow with the journey of our soul and receive the gifts and teachings of this journey. When we walk in fearlessness, we are in balance; we are in integrity. We are in harmony for we are in ayni. There is no fear draining our energy. When we walk without fear, we walk in peace, for all is perfect as it is.

Manifest Reality

The sages know there is nothing holding us back from creating and manifesting a new reality—a reality that is of our dreams and that will support the manifestation of these dreams. A reality that some will say is impossible.

The sages know that nothing is impossible. They know that impossibility is just the manifestation of a myth or belief we have yet to release.

The sages know when we stop engaging with the myths and beliefs that no longer support our reality, we may create a new reality. A reality sourced from the void, the unmanifest energy of creation. Energy from which all that has not been may be brought forth to manifest in time and form. They know this with certainty.

The sages also know that when we no longer need to engage the myths and beliefs that have kept us unsafe, we may face the fears that live within us. These are the fears of certainty and uncertainty, the fears of change or the fear of achieving our greatest potential. This may even be the fear of being alive. When we bring these fears into awareness, we may honor and release them.

Once these beliefs are brought into awareness, heard, and honored, the power they hold over us in the form of doubt, uncertainty, and fear is transformed. When we have transcended these states of being, we are no longer held back by the fears that have haunted us.

We Can Just Be or Not Be

When we no longer need to change or do something, we can just be or not be. When there are no forces pulling or pushing us to be elsewhere, all is in balance. When all is perfect as it is, then we can just be present in the moment to experience life. Our wounding and our need to heal our fears are no longer a distracting force.

The sages know being present to experience any moment in life is a gift the universe has orchestrated to support our growth. They know that through the experience of adversity or turmoil we may access the teachings we must embody and the lessons we must learn to bring forth the healing of our soul. The sages know this with certainty; there is no doubt. There is no victim's voice seeking to be heard.

The sages know that when we walk in certainty, when we walk in fearlessness, when we no longer engage adversity, and when we have given up the need of doing, the universe will support us right where we are on our journey of life.

Like a Child

When we release our judgments, attachments, and stories of what has been and what can be, the sages say that we may once again experience life like a child. No longer do we prejudge an experience that has yet to occur based on the memories of our past. We experience each moment, each breath, and each space between the breaths as if for the first time. Like a child, we experience life through the eyes of innocence and through a lens untainted by life.

When we are totally present, we become aware of how each breath, each thought we have, affects not just ourselves but all of creation. When we are totally present, we become aware that our thoughts, beliefs, actions, and compassion create our world, our reality.

The sages know our thoughts are energy, and that our thoughts affect who we are and who we say we are. They know that our thoughts affect our children, our community, and create our reality. The sages know when we step out of ayni, out of integrity, with ourselves, our community, or with Spirit, we create a reality in which illness, disease, and turmoil can occur.

We realize to have integrity, to be in harmony, we must honor all aspects of ourselves, the good, the bad, and the ugly. The sages tell us that even our demons, our shadow, and our enemies are to be honored, for they are manifestations of ourselves and manifestations of Spirit. They tell us when we dishonor the demons, the enemies, or our shadow, we dishonor ourselves. We dishonor Spirit.

Masters of Time

The sages say we become masters of time when we no longer judge an experience that has yet to occur based on the experience of the past. They know that when we step from the grips of time, we may experience infinity.

In infinity, synchronicity becomes the governing principle. Events are no longer governed by cause and effect or by the fear of what might happen. In infinity, all can occur. Time becomes circular. The past informs the future. The future informs the past. The impossible becomes possible.

In infinity, the sages tell us we no longer need to make something happen, for in the divine timing of life, it either happens or it does not. All is perfect as it is.

The sages know when we step out of linear time, we become the observer. We no longer blindly write the story of suffering or of victimhood. We see the opportunity for growth and for healing. We know the universe has provided us with exactly what we can handle to allow our soul to grow and evolve.

In infinity, we take ownership of our life; we own our thoughts, beliefs, and judgments. We take responsibility for dreaming our world into being. We become the author of our own story. We no longer hold others responsible for our unhappiness or for our life's circumstances.

In infinity, we see the opportunity to step into wholeness and into right relationship with ourselves, our community, and with Spirit. In infinity, we no longer strive to be in ayni; we no longer see ayni as a concept or way of life. We become ayni. We become one with self, with our community, and with Spirit. In infinity, we are ayni.

Choice

We have choices in life. When we choose to embody the wisdom teachings, we choose to live in fearlessness, peace, and awareness. In fearlessness, we welcome the gifts and opportunity for growth that life presents to us, even those gifts delivered in the guise of illness or disease.

When presented with a gift of misfortune, we have the choice to look at the wrapping of this gift and be disempowered. Or, we have the choice to unwrap the gift and discover what is held within the wrappings. The wisdom keepers choose to unwrap the gift, to discover the myths, the stories, and the opportunities it holds.

They know the wrapping is only the consensual reality of the masses, a reality they may wish not to accept. We, too, may unwrap the gift of misfortune to discover the opportunities held for us within its wrappings. When we make this choice to discover the meaning and purpose of misfortune that comes into our life, we become empowered.

Awareness, Access to the Inner Healer

To access our inner healer and change our reality, we must first desire change. We do not change for our family, friends, or boss. We change because we desire to be in right relationship with ourselves, our community, and with Spirit. We change because we desire to be in flow with the power of the universe. When we practice the wisdom teachings, the force and power of the universe support us on this journey through life.

When the wisdom teachings become not a practice but a way of life, our life changes; we live in synchronistic time, a time that is circular and sacred. Within this time, linear time exists, but it is not the controlling factor. We plant a seed, and if all things in sacred time conspire on behalf of the seed, the seed will sprout.

Awareness is essential for our journey of wholeness. Awareness allows access to the inner shaman, the voice of the healer within each of us. It is this voice to whom, when we listen, our body, mind, and soul attune to create the conditions for health and wholeness to manifest. When we listen to the voice of this inner healer, we hear the calling of our soul and know our path to joy and beauty.

Once we have awareness, we have free choice. With awareness, we can make conscious choices. With awareness, the unconscious becomes conscious. With awareness and consciousness, we can make the life choices that bring us into ayni, into balance with ourselves, our community, and with Spirit.

With awareness, we can be free of suffering; we can choose to practice non-suffering. With awareness, we can be free of judgment; we can choose to practice non-judgment. With awareness, we can be free of attachment; we can choose to practice non-attachment. With awareness, we practice certainty. We practice non-doing. We practice beauty.

With awareness, we become aware of who we are, not how others desire us to be. With awareness, we see through the myths that have created a reality that we can now choose to change. With awareness, we may create new myths that support a reality of joy and beauty, a reality of compassion and peace, or a reality of health and balance. With awareness, we create a reality of love and life, supported by the wisdom teachings and the way of ayni.

With Awareness Comes Choice

With awareness comes choice. When we embody the wisdom teachings, how we live life becomes a choice. How we perceive and how we respond to events in our life becomes a choice. When we embody the wisdom teaching, we become the creator of our own myths, beliefs, and reality.

Let us look at our daily life. What is blocking or stopping us from living in awareness? What are the stories and beliefs we tell about ourselves during the day? When we look at a mirror, who do we see? How do we live the life that others have assigned us? How do we live the roles, labels, and judgments others have attached to us or to our life?

Why have we agreed to these roles and labels? Why have we agreed to be a victim, to live in the triangle of disempowerment? This triangle depletes the energy we could use to discover our true essence, energy we could use to call forth and manifest the destiny we desire for our journey.

Awareness, Desire, and Transformation

The transformational power of awareness and desire is a key element in creation of a new reality. Desire speaks of a need to be different or to have something else. Desire is a strong motivational force in support of transformation. When we call upon the motivational force of desire to help us create a new reality, we must do so with full awareness of our desire. We must ask and know, "Whose desire is it for me to be different? Whose myths have I been living? Who has created this need for me to be different?" and "For whom do I walk this journey of transformation?"

When we do not first answer these questions, we will create new myths that support an old reality—a reality that was created by others or by the unconscious myths and beliefs we have lived without question. Today with clear vision and through the lens of wholeness and of health, let us create the myths that will support our myths of creation and the reality of our choice.

Unconscious Triggers and Beliefs

We react consciously and unconsciously to events and situations we encounter. Our conscious awareness is most likely based on unconscious triggers that have been embedded into our luminous field of energy. These embedded packets of energy are like the icons on a computer screen; when triggered, they activate hidden programs that in conjunction with the operating system of our home computer produce a reaction. These embedded triggers are known as imprints. Imprints predispose us to circumstances and patterns of behavior. We may experience illness, disease, or turmoil as a result of an imprint that has formed within our energetic field.

Imprints are formed in the energetic matrix of our body when a traumatic event occurs and is not healed or processed at the time of its occurrence. The trauma may have been real or imagined. The mind really does not care. The experience of a perceived traumatic event is real to the mind and despite evidence to the contrary continues to be real until healing occurs.

A child left unattended by his caretaker may experience an imprint that subjects him to fears of abandonment throughout his life. How the child responds to this event, whether as a great adventure or as a threat to survival, will determine if an imprint is formed.

Should an imprint be formed, the child left unattended might, as an adult, suffer from extreme anxiety when the age-appropriate process of individuation occurs for their own children. Or as an adult, this child might experience feelings of unworthiness or abandonment when their partner desires time alone. While modern psychology might attribute such behaviors to anxious attachment and treat the behavioral symptoms, the shamanic approach would be to clear the imprint associated with the traumatic event.

When We Practice the Wisdom Teachings

The sages tell us when we practice the wisdom teachings, how we live life becomes a choice. How we perceive and how we respond to events becomes a choice.

The sages also tell us when we choose to explore the depths of our shadows and the cause of our reactions, we will live life in awareness. We will remember who we are and know our authentic self.

The sages say when we know our authentic self, we are free to weave the myths of creation that support the dreams and manifestation of a new reality. A reality in which we are in right relationship with all that is. A reality of ayni in which all that we are experiencing is perfect as is.

CHAPTER FOUR

THE JOURNEY OF SHAMANIC HEALING

The Journey to Health

Healing is a journey of our soul. A journey that transcends the life we are living. It is the dance that brings our spirit into harmony and balance with all that is or is not. The journey of healing allows our soul to thrive, to grow, and to evolve no matter where we are on the journey of life. It is the path we walk as our soul journeys to that realm of being where we are once again in right relationship with self, community, and Spirit.

On this journey as we embody the teachings of the wisdom keepers, we take responsibility for our life. We create new myths. Myths that will create new beliefs. Beliefs that may open us to a new reality, perhaps a reality of joy, beauty, and courage. A reality where, with compassion, we may forgive ourselves or others for what was said or not said, done or not done. This may be a reality that allows us, perhaps for the first time in our life, to experience the gifts of peace and tranquility or of abundance and balance.

On this journey we remember. We remember the journey to health begins with a whisper that becomes louder until the call cannot be avoided. We remember this journey is one of awareness and of choice. We remember there are four parts of this journey: the calling, the departure, the tests, and the return. We remember this is a journey of honoring and of release. It is a journey of transformation and of transcendence. It is a journey of death and of creation.

It is a journey upon which we remember the archetypal energies of the cosmos are here, ready to assist us as we walk this path of health. A path we travel as we journey through the realms of the known and the unknown.

Shamanic Healing Offers Us a Map

Shamanic healing offers us a map for the journey to wholeness and health. But it is only a map. The journey is ours to walk. And we must walk alone. The journey may lead us into deep canyons, across deserts, or through treacherous ravines. On this journey we may meet the source of our greatest fears or the demons of our own creation.

As we embark on this journey of understanding and integration, we may find the insights and provisions offered within the pages of this book to be of service, in fact essential for the completion of this journey. These gifts of wisdom and insight will provide us with a compass and a map of the land that we will walk.

On this journey we may choose to embody the wisdom teachings of the sages—teachings that will allow us to transform and transcend the demons of our creation into our greatest allies and teachers. The same teachings that will bring clear vision and guidance as we create a world in which we are in harmony with all that is. The journey is ours to take. No one can take this journey for us.

A Word of Caution

Along this path, there may be an oasis where we may be nourished and where we may rest. But we must not be seduced by the comforting waters; we must not tarry long. The oasis may only be a mirage that lures us into complacency as we walk this journey of health.

CHAPTER FIVE

"VOICES OF THE CANYON"

There are voices that, when we choose to listen, we hear. These are the voices of nature, which speak to us when we stop and listen. I returned to Esalen in February 2015. As I walked the canyons and connected to the lands of Esalen, I chose to stop. I chose to listen. This is what I heard.

These are the voices of the Canyon,

The voices of the wind, the trees, the stones,
The voices of the rock walls, the rushing stream, the deep pools.

These are the voices of the Canyon.

It is a process of blossoming, of opening, of revelation, of revealing oneself.
It is a process of transformation and of shifting shapes.

Today I am a tree, tomorrow a stone or a human.

The transition may be turbulent like rapids or still like a deep pond.

What appears as chaos is finely orchestrated by the universe.

The narrow bridge we walk one at a time is our transition to a new form, a new shape. Perhaps to a new reality, a new consciousness.

Do we dare to look back, to remember from where we came, or do we move forward to explore the untapped possibility of the universe?

What fed us, what nourished us, what made us who we were—we are not that one any longer.

What now feeds us, what now nourishes us, what now sustains us? What now shapes our reality?

Where do we dig beneath, crawl beneath the obstacles?
Where do we fly over these obstacles?
Where do we rest? Where do we integrate the changes?

With whom do we catch a ride, and where, where do we hop off to walk alone, again?

The waters that feed us, that hydrate us, spring forth from the source, from the face of the stone wall.

We squeeze through the narrow canyon of transformation to rest by a sacred pond to grow, to evolve.

Do we stop and rest, or move forward, called by the end, not by the journey? The journey of joy, of beauty, and of the experiences along the way.

Breathe, breathe, then don't breathe.
Receive the beauty, the joy, and the love of the moment.
This is the gift of the universe, the gift to our soul.

As we return along the path, the lands are similar, but our soul has shifted. It has been dismembered and remembered along the way.

We have returned to where we began this journey, but the soul who has returned is not the soul that began the journey.

We are no longer defined by the one we were, the one who we remembered, the one who we released, or the one who we honored.

We are now the one we picked up and gave voice to along the way.

The one whose faint voice has called us, whose faint voice we answered, the one who will lead us on the next phase of our journey.

My journey began in the gardens of Esalen. There was a whisper that I heard that stormy weekend in 2006, a whisper that became a calling, a knowing. I returned a decade later to where this part of the journey began. I heard the voices of the canyon that day.

As you embark upon the journey, I encourage you to take the time to stop, to integrate, and to listen for the voices of nature. For those who do stop and listen, there will be a gift—a gift of transformation and transcendence, a gift of mystery and unknowing. I leave you with one final thought about the journey, as told to me by the canyons.

"Unlike"

Unlike the others who have walked before,
Unlike the others who have walked before,
He chose to listen; he chose to speak.
Unlike the others who have walked before.

****

I thank the creative voices of the void that have brought forth this story of integration and understanding.

POSTSCRIPT

Our Personal Map

We have a map of our journey through life. On this map, we have the coordinates of where and who we are today. We have an awareness of the roles we have played, of the beliefs and the myths that we have carried on this journey, and the gods we have served and who have served us.

We may be quite happy and comfortable where we are, and if so, we may choose to remain, finding no need or desire to experience other realities or other gods. Perhaps we are uncertain, without a vision or awareness of our desires or the journey we walk. If this is the case, for now just allow the self to sit in stillness and be. This may be a time to lie fallow in the fields of creation.

It Is When

It is when we are restless, when we hear the whispers of discontent in our current reality. It is when we can sense there is something more in life; something more to be discovered and experienced. It is then that we realize the need for a new map. A map that will lead us from where we are into new lands and new territories. A map that can orient and guide us along the path to a new destination.

It has been said that we are the cartographers of our life, that we create the topography of our journey, the mountains, the deserts, streams, and canyons we encounter as we move through life. It is from where we focus as the cartographer that life is created, and it is from this point of focus that life is judged and experienced. When we focus on what is wrong with our lives, what we are lacking and what we are missing, it will not matter if we have created new maps, for we will find the same topography no matter where we are standing. We will find mountains that are too steep. We will find deserts too barren, rivers too swift, and canyons too deep.

But what if, instead, we focused upon a journey that held the possibilities of life? The possibilities of joy and beauty, the possibilities of abundance and balance, or the possibilities of wholeness and health. A journey of new lands and uncharted territory. Lands and territories that we may have no way to envision or to access, only a sense of their essence and what they may hold for us. It is this essence, this sense of mystery we wish to capture, manifest, and anchor within our energetic field as we begin to draw the new maps and construct the bridges that will allow us to transition into new realms of being.

If There Is a Vision

Let us take a moment and begin to energize the possibilities we wish to bring forth. If there is a vision, what would the maps and the topography of these lands be like? Are there trails that take us through or around the steep mountains? Is there an oasis that will offer us water and nourishment in the barren deserts?

What are the myths that will support this vision? Are they myths of worthiness, compassion, abundance, or ability? What are the beliefs we must hold that will create a strong foundation for the bridges and that will lay down the paths that did not previously exist so we may transition to a new realm of being?

Remember, we are the cartographer; we may create these new lands, this new reality as we desire. We might ask, "What if I experience love or beauty? How would I feel, how would I know?" Then we let the imagination choregraph this new sense of being and possibility without judgment or attachment to past belief or experience.

We may download to our soul the coordinates for health and for wholeness. We may orient and calibrate our inner compass to bring forth the possibilities of life we have yet to discover, experience, or even imagine possible. These may be the realms of love, joy, or courage. They may manifest subtly in the etheric or perhaps physically in the form of a rose or of a hummingbird that brings warmth to the heart.

Throughout This Guide

Throughout this guide, we have been enlightened, we have received clarity, and we have received vision as to who and why we are. We have let go of the maps and bridges of others that would guide us to their dreams and desires. We have remembered our salka self, and who we desire to be. We have worked in ceremony. We understand the value of ritual.

We have called upon the primordial energies of the medicine wheel and of the archetypes of creation. We have brought ourselves into harmony with the gods and learned to work with the elements of the earth, the sky, the waters, and fire. We have been gifted the wisdom teachings of the elders. We have heard the voices of the canyons. Now, let us take this clarity, this wisdom, this vision, and the tools we have been gifted along the way and use them to create the maps and the bridges of the journey. These maps will take us to the lands of our dreams and desires manifested.

As we begin our journey, as we call forth the essence of our dreams, we may once again face the fears and voices of our own making, or the voices of the naysayers who claim our dream is not possible. These are the voices that say we are not worthy; we are not deserving to have what we desire.

We remember these voices of fear and of doubt are a gift. They are the tests that will strengthen our resolve and bring deeper clarity and understanding as to the journey we are walking. An opportunity perhaps to revisit our shadow, to honor and own those pieces of ourselves that we have not seen. Or we may find this an opportunity to further refine the myths, beliefs, and roles that are defining who we are and who we are becoming. We may even find this an opportunity to create an updated vision statement that guides and nourishes our soul as we move forward through life.

At Times We May Need Ask

At times we may need to ask of our self and of our soul, are we where we desire to be on this map of creation? If yes, wonderful. If no, then what needs to change in the foundation of our myths and beliefs to bring us to where we desire to be today or next year?

Let us take a moment to connect with the essence of our dreams and the possibilities of our journey. As we envision this journey: What resources and nourishment will we require to build the bridge or provide us sustenance along the way? Once we have crossed the bridge and arrived into new lands, what will be needed to grow and anchor our roots firmly into the soils of these lands?

We may wish to create a list of the provisions and resources that we already have or that we will need to acquire for this journey. These may be in the form of new behaviors, myths, or beliefs. We may be required to allow what we had envisioned and held dearly as truths to die so that we may bring forth new truths and new possibilities. We may see times of rest to allow for integration to occur along the way.

Let us make note of these needs and allow our soul to know where these provisions and resources are stockpiled, waiting and available to provide the required nourishment and sustenance for our journey.

Let Us Bring Forth

Now let us bring forth the essence of a bridge from the unmanifest energy of creation. A bridge of strong foundation and expansive reach that will carry us into new realms of being. A bridge that will allow us to transition from where we are now into the new lands we have envisioned.

We may use crayons or colored pencils to draw this bridge or paste images from a magazine to bring forth the essence of this bridge into a material form. We allow this essence to inform our soul and our creation. We do this without judgment, without attachment to the outcome of the drawings or images. We allow the form to flow from our soul, not from the judgments of our mind.

When You Are Ready

When you are ready, I invite you to visualize as you cross this bridge. A bridge that will carry you from your current reality into the realms of manifested dreams and possibilities. A bridge across which you may take the first steps of the journey to health and wholeness.

Once you have visualized this journey and your soul knows the way, allow the physical body to participate. Find a bridge that spans a river or perhaps a busy highway. Then with intent begin this journey of health and wholeness as you literally take the first step across this bridge into the mystery of life and possibility.

Some may desire to do this crossing in a ceremony, witnessed by others. Some may wish this journey to start in solitude, taking the first step at the edge of a field where no path has existed before. However this journey is undertaken, upon completion, take time to honor the journey and celebrate the one who has taken these steps.

APPENDIX

As we process the material of this book, we are doing deep energetic work. It may be helpful to use the tools and practices below to assimilate and integrate the healing that is occurring in the energetic field. These are suggestions that I offer clients after a session to assist in the integration of their healing work.

The Effect of Shamanic Healing

Disturbances in the human energy field created by unresolved trauma, by conflict within our life, or by our personal beliefs and thoughts may lead to physical disease, illness, or emotional turmoil. Once the energetic field and chakras have been cleansed, attuned, and balanced, the structure of this energetic matrix immediately shifts, providing the opportunity for health, harmony, and wholeness to occur within body, mind, spirit, and soul.

The effect of shamanic healing occurs first in the field of energy that surrounds our physical body. This field of energy holds the blueprints for the emotional and physical bodies. It is within these blueprints that the trauma of unhealed wounds may create illness, turmoil, or disease in our life. This is our personal field of energy. It is a matrix upon which our physical and emotional body takes form. It is the matrix that provides the vessel in which our soul resides in this life.

While the changes that occur in the matrix of this energetic field are immediate, the resultant changes in the mind and physical body may take several days, weeks, or months to fully integrate and manifest. During this time old neuropathways are extinguished, and new pathways are created.

After Your Session

After your session you may experience a sense of well-being and harmony. There may be a sense of leaving something behind or a sense of wholeness. You may feel full of energy or have the desire to rest. There may be a sense of joy or sadness, tears or laughter, for no apparent reason. Let the experience occur. This is the energy continuing to release and balance. The rituals and ceremonies described below will help to integrate and deepen the healing that occurred today.

Journal

Journal. Write about your session while it is still fresh. What did you experience today? Were there images, thoughts, or awareness that came to you? Some individuals experience healing colors, shapes, or guides that appear to them.

How do you feel different? Do you feel a weight has been lifted, a lightness of being, or a sense that cannot yet be put into words? Perhaps there is just a knowing or understanding of what is. Return to the journal over the next several weeks and months, reviewing and adding whatever comes up for you.

Nourishment

Nourishment on all levels of your body is important to facilitate the integration of your healing process. During this process of healing, we wish to attend to the physical body, the mind, the soul, and the luminous field of energy that surrounds us.

1. Rest.
2. Drink plenty of fluids.
3. Take time to connect with nature and to the energies of Mother Earth.
4. Receive daily nourishment from the sun and from nature.
5. Practice meditation and visualization.
6. Indulge in that which nourishes your soul (music, books, art, poetry, nature).
7. Eat healthfully.

8. Avoid excessive alcohol usage.
9. Avoid recreational drugs.
10. Practice awareness.
    a. Become aware of your thoughts. What do you focus on each day? How does this focus feed or nourish you?
    b. Through awareness we may see how we handle the stresses in our life, or we may assess the personal habits of our lifestyle and beliefs. Do we exercise each day? Do we connect with the energies of nature? Do we take time to meditate or find stillness each day?

Baths

Baths may be healing as well as nourishing.
1. Salt bath
    a. Taking a salt bath helps to continue the release of heavy energy from the luminous body.
    b. To prepare the bath add one-half cup of sea salt or Epsom salts, plus one-half cup of baking soda to the bathwater.
    c. Soak for fifteen minutes.
    d. Use this time to meditate or just be in silence.
    e. Candles and relaxing music may help facilitate the process.
2. Flower bath
    a. Later that night or the following day, draw a second bath with fresh water.
    b. Add flower petals or essential oils to this second tub of water to feed and nourish your soul.
    c. Certain fragrances may nurture you; add these to the water.
    d. Candles, music, and incense may also facilitate the healing and nourishing of your soul.
    e. Allow your soul to be nourished.

Chakra Cleansing

Take time each week to cleanse your chakras. You may perform the cleansing as you shower or as you lie quietly in your bed. Begin by taking a deep, cleansing breath in through your nose and out through your mouth. Next, locate your first chakra at the base of the spine.

Unwind and backwash this chakra by placing the fingers of your right hand in the mouth of the chakra and spinning counter-clockwise ten times. You may wish to visualize pure white light entering each chakra as you cleanse it. To complete the process, spin the chakra in a clockwise rotation. Repeat this process for each of the seven chakras.

If you are not sure of the location of your chakras, do a Google search for an image of their location.

Create a Ceremony

Create a ceremony to honor the healing you have done today. It is also important to honor the past and what you have released. Be creative. Allow this ceremony to reflect your journey. This ceremony may be very simple or elegant. Listen to your soul's desire.

Fire Ceremony

The fire ceremony is a ceremony that can be used to release the heavy energies and limiting beliefs that are bound within us, and to bring forth and germinate the seeds of our new beliefs and dreams.

To perform a fire ceremony, you will need a stick and a source of fire. Open sacred space. Light a candle or create a fire outdoors in a container. Set your intent to release the beliefs and judgments that are blocking your emotional body, your physical body, and your energetic body from healing. Close your eyes. Take two or three deep breaths and follow your breath as it carries you into a beautiful meadow.

Become aware how Mother Earth embraces and holds you. This is the mother who will never leave you. Feel the warmth of the sun as it nourishes you. This is the father who will never abandon you. Allow your breath to circulate through your physical body, your emotional body, your soul, and your energetic body, finding what needs to be released. Just let it happen.

Your breath knows what needs to be released. Now pick up the stick. Again, use your breath. Blow into the stick as many times as necessary to completely release the energy from your body and into the stick. Place the stick into the fire. Watch as the stick transforms into smoke, light, and ash.

After the stick has burned, pass your hand through the smoke of the fire or the candle, and bring the light of this fire into your belly, your heart, and your forehead. These are the three main energy centers of the body. From your heart, honor and thank the energy you released. Then allow your breath to bring you back home.

Symbolically, the wind (your breath) carries the energy that was once bound within out of the body and into the stick. Once this energy is blown into the stick, the stick is no longer a stick. It is the emotion or the belief to be transformed. The fire then releases the energy contained in the stick and transforms the energy into pure light.

What was once bound within you, blocking your journey, has been removed, transformed. The light is now available to feed, nourish, and guide you along your path. It is this light, this energy, that is brought into the three main energy centers of the body, the belly, the heart, and the forehead. This energy is the energy of creation and all possibility.

Sand Painting

Another form of transformative ceremony is the sand painting. When you create a sand painting (or mandala), you are working at the mythic, at the level of the soul. The sand painting represents you. It is a mirror of who you are. At the energetic there is no difference between you and the image created in the painting. A sand painting allows the issues to be processed outside of the physical or emotional body. The changes that occur in the sand painting will create change and transformation within your body.

A sand painting is made outside on the earth, but if that is not possible, find a space inside your home (a pie pan filled with soil or sand works). Collect sticks, stones, and other objects found in nature or other items that have special meaning to you. Later these will be placed in the sand painting to represent the beliefs and issues that are blocking the path of your healing.

To create the sand painting, open sacred space (see below). Then with the intent of capturing the essence of your spirit, create a circle on the ground. This circle represents a vessel to hold the energy of your spirit. The border of the circle may be made by drawing a circle in the dirt or creating a border with sticks and stones. Select a stone.

Blow the essence of who you are into this stone and anchor it firmly into the center of the circle. Next, set your intent to release from your emotional body, physical body, and energetic body the beliefs and judgments that are blocking you from healing. Pick up one of the objects you selected from nature. Take two or three deep breaths. Blow whatever comes up for you into the object and place it into the sand painting. You will know where this object is to be placed within the circle. You may do this for up to three issues.

Visit the sand painting at least daily. See what changes have occurred. Make changes if it feels right. Perhaps a flower needs to cover an issue to bring healing, or a stone representing a weighty issue no longer holds a charge, so it can be removed from the sand painting. You may wish to journal about your thoughts and the lessons you are learning. The sand painting can stay active for about a week, but it may do its work in a shorter period of time.

Trust yourself. You will sense when it is done working for you. Return the items back to nature or burn them in a sacred fire. Close sacred space. When you leave, there should be no evidence that a sand painting was there.

Altars

Altars are another form of ceremony. An altar might be made to honor relatives, deceased ancestors, or a stage of life that has ended.

Choose a special place in your home (other than your bedroom, where the veils between the realms are thin) to create this altar. The altar may consist of pictures of you at an earlier age or of deceased relatives. It may contain items from nature or of special meaning to you. Follow your inner guidance as to what should be placed there.

The altar is not for worship but for honoring. Honoring is an important practice and essential for stepping into a healed state. Honoring does not mean condoning the hurt that might have occurred. Honoring is a process of acknowledging an event or person without judgment. It is a place of release and of forgiveness. Honoring allows the situation to find its neutral place, that place of no energetic charge, emotional or otherwise.

Prayer Bundle

A prayer bundle is a vessel to bring our prayers and desires to Spirit and the universe. The first step is to offer our gratitude to all of creation for what we have. We place our intent for health, gratitude, or our future into this bundle. We place our intent for what we wish to manifest in life, not for what we are lacking or feel entitled to. Upon completion it is offered to Spirit and the universe.

The prayer bundle can be as simple as a collection of burnable items (leaves, twigs, etc.) brought together in a paper bag where you have blown your essence, your prayers, your gratitude, and your dreams. This may be mixed with incense or sweet herbs whose fragrances will carry our dreams and the offerings of our gratitude to Spirit. The essence of our prayers is released to the universe as it is transformed by the elements, either offered through fire ceremony or through burial in the earth. The prayer bundle may also be tossed into the ocean or a river, or carried by the strength of the wind.

Stone Cleansing

Find a stone that calls to you. Keep this stone near you. When issues or feelings arise, blow these energies into the stone. It may take as few as five breaths or more than twenty-five breaths to release this energy. Continue to blow the energy you wish to release into the stone until it is gone. To cleanse this stone, place it on the ground or in the earth overnight and let Mother Earth take the energies.

You might also place a stone over the area of concern within your body, and allow the energy or blockages to be drawn from your body and into the stone. After, you may give the stone and the energy that was removed back to Mother Earth, who will transform this energy into nourishment and sustenance that will be available to feed you along the course of your journey of health and wellness.

Release to Mother Earth

Another method to release heavy energy is to release it to the earth through your first chakra, the root chakra. Visualize a column of light that extends from your first chakra, located at the base of your spine, deep into Pachamama, Mother Earth. Allow her to receive the heavy energies (the emotions, the thoughts you desire not to have) that are being held in the layers of your body. Use your breath and your intent to carry this heavy energy from your body and through the channel to Mother Earth. It will be received graciously and mulched by the earth and returned as nourishment and sustenance to your body.

Simultaneously open the seventh chakra, at the crown of the head. From this point extend a column of light to the heavens, to Spirit, or to wherever you source from and allow the pure energy of creation, of all possibilities, to flow through all the layers of your body and luminous energy field. This energy of creation will feed and inform who you are becoming.

Body Awareness

Sense in your body where the issue or story lives. It may be a chronic pain, a pressure that develops as you think of the issue or event, or just an intuitive awareness. Take a stick and with a counterclockwise motion imagine that you are pulling this energy, this blockage out from your body. It may be like a thread that courses through or around your body or even to an ancestor. Place this energy in a fire and let it transform.

Once it is gone, become aware. Sense the space that has been opened to allow growth and healing to occur. Create an image of beauty, peace, or health. Allow this image to fill the space that you have now created.

Sound

Is there a sound that needs to be released from your body? Let it out. Let it all the way out from your cells, your organs, and your core.

Songs of Life

Through awareness we may create songs of joy and peace, songs of wholeness and health, or songs of love and light. Awareness allows us free will to create these songs of life. What are the songs of life you desire to create? To bring forth these songs, we may need to ask these or similar questions first:

a. What needs to change in my life?
b. Where is my life out of balance? Where am I out of integrity with myself or with others?
c. What are the stories that feed my beliefs about the world in which I live? Whose stories, whose beliefs are these?
d. How am I the creator of my life? What are the roles I have created, and what are my beliefs or myths of reality?
e. Have I created roles of victimhood or of empowerment?
f. What is the lesson that this situation can teach me?
g. Why do these issues keep showing up in my life?

h. What is my opportunity for growth or learning as a result of what is going on in my life? What may be the gift of this illness?

i. What if I were not caught up in the drama of my suffering or my story? What would I do instead? Who would I be? How could I use my energy to create what I truly desire?

When you have found the new song in your body, give it voice. Sing it out loud. Let your body, your cells, your organs resonate with this new sense of freedom, of empowerment, of ...

Sacred Space

Shamans always work within sacred space. This is a vessel, a container of sacred vibrations and energy. If you do nothing else, immerse and bathe yourself in the energies and vibration of this sacred container.

The invocation found below is my adaptation of the invocation offered and generously shared by Alberto Villoldo. Use this invocation as you please to create a personal healing space in which you may be held and nourished. As you create this vessel, turn toward the direction of the spirits you are addressing and recite the appropriate paragraph.

When you are ready to close the space, thank and release the directions, Mother Earth, and Father Sun.

To the winds of the South, great serpent
Wrap your coils of light around us
Teach us to shed our past, as you shed your skin
We thank you for your gifts of wisdom, of knowledge, of healing, and
of fertility in all that we undertake.

To the winds of the West, mother sister jaguar, Otorongo
Come, come and protect our medicine space
Bring us the strength and the courage to walk this path
Teach us to walk in peace and with impeccability
Allow us to see what must die both within and outside so that the
new may be born.

To the winds of the North, siwar Q'enti hummingbird, grandmothers, grandfathers, ancient ones, come and warm your hands by our fire, whisper to us in the wind.

We honor those who have come before us and those who will come after, our children's children.

We thank you for your gifts of growth and evolution. We thank you as our soul reconnects with the songs of the cosmos and we remember our sacred journey.

To the winds of the East, great eagle, condor
You who have come from the place of the rising sun,
Who brings forth the newness of each day, and the energies of possibility.

You, who have taken us under your wings to teach us to fly wingtip to wingtip with Spirit. And have allowed us to soar above ourselves, to see with great vision and breath. We thank you. We thank you for your gifts of vision, clarity, foresight, transformation, and Transcendence.

Mother Earth, we come for the healing of all. The stone people, the plant people, the four-legged, the two-legged, the finned, the furred, the creepy crawlers, all of creation and all of your children.

We thank you for this vessel, this foundation you have created to allow us to journey this path of life.

Father Sun, Inti Taita, Grandmother Moon, Mama Killa, star nations, star brothers, star sisters, yapan chaskakuna, yapan apukuna, Apu Ausangate, Apu Salkantay, Apu Huamalipa, Apu Whitney, all the sacred mountains come, come and be with us. Healers of all lineages. Mamma Coccha, mother of the Waters, Creator, Creatrix, you who are of one energy, great Spirit, thank you for allowing us to be here as we walk once again as one.

In Conclusion

Please note, the exercises and resources above will assist in the process and integration of the energetic release and shifts that occurred during your session. While many may experience a permanent sense of well-being immediately after a session, occasionally one might experience a sense of loss, sadness, or grief that is the result of residual energy, or from the stimulation of cellular memories associated with the removal of these energies. This is normal if it occurs and usually will resolve within a few hours or days. There are, however, times and places along this journey to abundance, joy, balance, harmony, and health that you may find it helpful to process the changes that are occurring in your life with a therapist or counselor.

Remember, when we have learned the lessons and taken control of our life, when we have become the creator of our own story, then healing will follow.

****

Shamanic healing is complementary to, not a replacement for, Western medicine. When under the care of a physician, do not stop or alter any therapy or prescription usage without first consulting the physician or health-care provider. It may also be appropriate to consult with a physician or therapist as you walk and process this journey.

****

ABOUT THE AUTHOR

Jim Dewell, a native of Southern California, is a graduate of Stanford University with a degree in Human Biology, and of The George Washington University School of Medicine.

Board Certified in the specialty of Family Medicine, Jim has taught medical students, trained residents entering the field of Family Practice and cared for his patients.

Jim is also a graduate and former senior faculty member of the Four Winds Society and Healing the Light Body School of Energy Medicine.

Under the cloak of illness and at the height of his medical career, Jim was visited by Spirit. It would be years however before Jim would or could understand the magnitude and impact of this visit or of the gift; a gift that changed his destiny. A gift of illness through which Spirit had taken Jim from the practice of medicine to fulfill his calling as a healer.

During Jim's shamanic apprenticeship, he studied under the tutelage of Alberto Villoldo, and with indigenous healers living in the jungles of the Amazon, the mountainous villages of the Andes, and throughout the Q'ero nation. Healers who graciously and with generosity shared their wisdom and understanding of life.

Made in United States
North Haven, CT
07 June 2022

19958787R00178